Debating
Single-Sex Education

Separate and Equal?

Edited by
Frances R. Spielhagen

Rowman & Littlefield Education
Lanham, Maryland • Toronto • Plymouth, UK
2008

Published in the United States of America
by Rowman & Littlefield Education
A Division of Rowman & Littlefield Publishers, Inc.
A wholly owned subsidary of
The Rowman & Littlefield Publishing Group, Inc.
4501 Forbes Boulevard, Suite 200, Lanham, Maryland 20706
www.rowmaneducation.com

Estover Road
Plymouth PL6 7PY
United Kingdom

British Library Cataloguing in Publication Information Available

Library of Congress Cataloging-in-Publication Data

Debating single-sex education : separate and equal? / edited by Frances R.
Spielhagen.
    p. cm.
 Includes bibliographical references.
 ISBN-13: 978-1-57886-737-0 (hardcover : alk. paper)
 ISBN-13: 978-1-57886-738-7 (pbk. : alk. paper)
 ISBN-10: 1-57886-737-1 (hardcover : alk. paper)
 ISBN-10: 1-57886-738-X (pbk. : alk. paper)
 1. Single-sex schools—United States. 2. Sex differences in education—
United States. I. Spielhagen, Frances R., 1946–
 LB3067.4.D43 2008
 371.82—dc22   2007037768

∞™ The paper used in this publication meets the minimum requirements of
American National Standard for Information Sciences—Permanence of Paper
for Printed Library Materials, ANSI/NISO Z39.48-1992.
Manufactured in the United States of America.

Contents

Foreword

Michael Gurian and Kathy Stevens

The work of the Gurian Institute and Dr. Frances R. Spielhagen intersect through the lens of gender. Our institute has been working with educators around the United States, helping them explore strategies designed to improve performance, reduce disciplinary referrals, and, overall, help both boys and girls experience success in school and in life. Like Dr. Spielhagen, we ask, "What role does gender play in education?" and "What educational environment best meets the needs of both girls and boys?" These questions lead often to another question: "Are single-sex classes better than coed classes?"

Depending on what philosophical position one holds on this latter topic, examples can be offered up as "proof" for all sides. Some research shows that girls learn best in all-girl classes; another reports that girls learn best from female teachers. Yet another study claims that boys learn best in all-boy classes and that boys learn best from all-male teachers. Still other research maintains that boys experience most success when they have the girls around to show them how to behave, and girls are pushed to be more competitive when they have boys around to push the envelope. Educators and parents are left with a seemingly endless supply of contradictory studies supporting a variety of diverse conclusions.

Dr. Spielhagen and her colleagues know that there is a pressing need for much more research—reliable, science based, well designed—to help us begin to truly assess what impact single-sex classes have on student performance, school culture, and institutional structure. As educators everywhere look for answers to close performance and gender gaps, reports of the success of single-sex classes spark some struggling schools to consider following suit. Too often, this decision is made with too much haste and too little preparation. The results can be disastrous for all concerned, causing the failure of an option that could have, exercised with strategic planning and implementation, been sound.

In this book, Dr. Spielhagen and her colleagues make a significant contribution to the dialogue. By sharing the experiences of teachers, administrators, and, most importantly, the students who have participated in single-sex pilot projects during middle school, this book answers some important questions and clearly delineates questions yet to be fully explored. The case studies detailed in these chapters should be read carefully by any school or district exploring implementation of single-sex options. The lessons learned by students, parents, teachers, and administrators, objectively shared here by the researchers, should factor into any planned implementation of a single-sex pilot.

Dr. Spielhagen has contributed her expertise as a member of the Advisory Board of the Gurian Institute for the past several years. She has shared with us wisdom and acumen gleaned from 40 years of teaching. Her experience in the classroom and her passion for the new teachers she trains at Mount Saint Mary College touch the lives of many boys and girls she will never even meet. This book will answer some important questions for people as yet unsure about the role single-sex education should play in the overall scheme of educating our sons and daughters. It will plant the seeds for more questions and challenge us all to keep looking for answers.

Single-Sex Classes
Everything That's Old Is New Again

Frances R. Spielhagen

INTRODUCTION

Reform often brings the educational community full circle to organizational structures that were common in former times. This is the case with single-sex classes. Throughout the early days of American education, throughout the 19th century and into the early years of the 20th century, single-sex classes were a common arrangement in secondary schools. In fact, coeducational classes are a relatively new development in American education and education in general.

During the Progressive Era, the disciples of John Dewey urged the creation of the comprehensive coeducational high school that would provide a wide range of courses to all students, as suited to their needs. Early feminists supported this reform because, in theory, these schools would provide access to the entire curriculum to all students, particularly girls, who had previously been afforded limited opportunities, particularly in math and science. In fact, in 1912 the superintendent of the Los Angeles schools maintained that the study of algebra had "caused many a girl to lose her soul" (Krug, 1964, p. 347). Therefore, coeducational high school classes were a welcome innovation to the early feminist community. Over the course of the 20th century, coeducational classes resulted in greater numbers of girls taking advanced mathematics and science courses and ultimately attending college.

However, when coeducational classes became the norm in academic subjects, schools in the United States routinely maintained single-sex physical education classes. In 1975 Title IX (Tyack & Hansot, 2002) legislation specifically forbade this option, because it frequently resulted in inequitable distribution of resources and facilities for all-girl physical education and athletic teams. Confused over both the spirit and the letter of Title IX, schools began to steer clear of single-sex classes in all subjects, although they were not globally forbidden by the law (Salomone, 2003). Schools that attempted to implement single-sex classes frequently fell prey to conflicts between policy makers and educators over ideology and resources, as well as concerns about equity and stereotypical attitudes (Datnow, Hubbard, & Conchas, 2001).

Rhetoric about the effectiveness of single-sex classes dominated the last years of the 20th century, with conflicting opinions over how much boys or girls benefited, if at all, by the arrangement. At the same time, education policy makers looked to single-sex classes as a solution for declining achievement in specific content areas, specifically mathematics and science for girls and language arts and reading for boys. The Baltimore City Public Schools successfully implemented all-boys classes in its elementary schools, from pre-kindergarten to 5th grade, to improve the academic achievement of black male students from female-headed single-parent households.

Early research (Steedman, 1985; Fennema & Carpenter, 1981; Lee & Bryk, 1986) focused on the benefits of single-sex arrangements to address declining mathematics achievement among girls. These works laid the foundation for Sadker and Sadker's (1994) landmark text on how schools shortchange girls. However, Gilson (1999) compared single-sex and coeducational arrangements among female middle school students in independent schools and found no significant differences in mathematics achievement, quantitative performance, or attitude toward mathematics in either arrangement. The American Association of University Women (1998), which initially endorsed single-sex classes, ultimately reversed its official stance as potentially damaging to the opportunities girls might be offered and thereby adversely affecting their achievement in all arenas. By the end of the 20th century, educational researchers, including Judith Kleinfeld (1999), began to express concern about achievement issues among boys. In 2005 Kleinfeld founded The Boys Project, a network of educators and other social science researchers whose intention is to address the crisis among boys in the United States and in other developed nations of the world.

In 2002 an amendment to No Child Left Behind legislation opened the door for schools to experiment with single-sex classes as a means of improving educational outcomes for all students. Such arrangements began to increase throughout the nation, reaching at least 241 in 2006 (Vu, 2006) according to Stateline, an organization that tracks educational changes across the nation. Leonard Sax (2005), a physician-psychologist who maintains that boys and girls are hard-wired differently and need different school arrangements, records the growth of single-sex schools on a Web site he has created (www.singlesexschools.org).

In 2003 the Office of Civil Rights immediately began reviewing arguments about the legality of single-sex classes. In 2006 the United States Department of Education confirmed the legality of single-sex arrangements, a decision that emerged in the midst of the proliferation of such classes. Around that same time, Dee (2006) released his findings that matching the gender of the students and the teacher promoted the achievement of the students. His finding was that boys achieve more with male teachers and girls achieve more with female teachers, but he did not unequivocally endorse single-sex education.

Educators in the international arena have also weighed in on the effectiveness of the single-sex classes. In Australia researchers concluded that such classes resulted in no significant difference in mathematics achievement among either boys or girls, but that girls fared better in single-sex English classes (Mulholland, Hanson, & Kaminski, 2004). However, in the Netherlands, a study (Van de Gaer, Pustjens, Van Damme, & DeMunter, 2004) that compared single-sex versus coeducational arrangements indicated that boys make greater progress in coeducational language classes, but not in mathematics, while girls in single-sex classes make progress in mathematics but not language. Confusing? It becomes even more complicated after looking at the complexity of scheduling issues in middle schools.

Assessing the effectiveness of single-sex classes is problematic. In the United States single-sex arrangements are often part of multifaceted educational reform, including changes in curriculum delivery. Very often, single-sex classes are established in middle schools to attempt to bolster declining achievement among students who are already in great personal and intellectual flux. Nevertheless, although it is difficult to attribute effectiveness and positive results to any one factor, specifically the segregation of students by their sex, single-sex arrangements can be examined and the results evaluated to get a greater sense of whether such arrangements are worthwhile.

OVERVIEW OF THE CHAPTERS

This book examines single-sex arrangements through many different lenses. Findings have been gathered from across the United States and in Africa in order to provide a deep and multifaceted understanding of a somewhat controversial arrangement. The authors of each chapter provide in-depth analyses of their experiences with real and recent single-sex classes.

In chapter 2, "Jumping into the Fray," Deborah E. Marks and C. Sloan Burns recount their experiences in scheduling single-sex classes in their middle school in the southeastern United States. Administrators in middle schools struggle to design student-friendly and productive organizational arrangements for students. For Marks and Burns, the actual scheduling of single-sex classes was accidental but proved to be serendipitous. Faced with a computer scheduling glitch that created single-sex classes, these seasoned administrators opted to maintain the single-sex arrangements. They chronicle how they managed these single-sex classes and how they handled the responses of parents, teachers, and students to the arrangement.

In chapter 3 Suzanne Schwarz-McCotter examines the points of view of teachers and administrators who were part of an initiative to start single-sex classrooms in an urban middle school. Offered incentives by the district's administration to implement the classes on a trial basis, the school piloted the program in the hopes that low-achieving students would show academic growth in single-sex classrooms. McCotter interviewed both the teachers of the 6th-, 7th-, and 8th-grade classes and the middle school administrators to explore their perspectives about the benefits and detriments of the initiative. The administrative decision to start the program only to gain incentives, without a vision or understanding, hindered the teachers' abilities to make the most of the situation. Effective leadership at the district level may have alleviated such problems.

Chapter 4 shifts the lens to the viewpoints of the students in a small urban middle school located in a larger rural geographic area. Frances R. Spielhagen gathered the perspectives of students in the 6th, 7th, and 8th grades in this school through surveys, interviews, and classroom observations. Single-sex classes worked for some students across all grades. Overall, the younger the students, the more likely they favored the arrangement. Sixth-grade students, both boys and girls, reported the greatest satisfaction. Seventh-grade boys were negatively disposed, while eighth-grade girls maintained that the single-sex classes were better for academic achievement but that they preferred to "be with the guys." The students were vocal and candid about their involvement in single-sex classes.

Preparation of teachers for teaching in single-sex classes is critical in the success of the reform. In chapter 5 Margaret Ferrara tackles the issues surrounding the assignment of teachers to single-sex classes in the complex environment of public middle schools in the United States. Teacher awareness of the differences in learning preferences among boys and girls emerged as a critical issue in providing for the success of these classes.

The potential of single-sex classes to increase student achievement is the focus of chapter 6. Frances R. Spielhagen examined the effects of single-sex classes on standardized test scores in a small middle school. She found specific gains in test scores among both boys and girls. She also explored the opinions of the adult stakeholders—parents and teachers—who responded to survey questions about the ways in which the students in this school reacted to single-sex classes and how the arrangement affected their academic performance.

In chapter 7 Peter Ferrara and Margaret Ferrara joined forces to examine the disciplinary issues in single-sex classes in a small middle school. They found marked differences in the disciplinary infractions encountered in single-sex classes as opposed to similar infractions among students in the mixed classes. They concluded that this area demands further attention because it addresses key issues in the education of young adolescents.

In chapter 8 Karen B. Rogers presents a comprehensive study of the effects of single-sex classes on middle school mathematics and science classes. She found substantial differences in classroom climate, instructional presentation, students' questioning/learning behaviors, and students' attitudes about single-gender and mixed-gender classes. Rogers's work also focuses on a specific segment of the student population: those who are highly able and are considered gifted.

Chapter 9 takes the question of single-sex classes to Africa, where Robin Kohl explains the ways in which these classes are organized in Kenya. Through her interviews with girls in that country, Kohl found that the girls in these classes were very motivated to achieve academically, routinely studying at least 6 hours every day. All of the students she interviewed indicated that they planned to postpone marriage and motherhood to attend university, with the majority of them interested in pursuing careers in law or economics.

Finally, Karen B. Rogers concludes with a summary of the implications of all of the work in this volume. In chapter 10 she provides the reader with a nexus of conclusions to be drawn from all the studies as well as the potential avenues for future research on this topic. Rogers also provides compelling implications and recommendations for practice in middle schools, where single-sex classes seem to have found a well-suited niche.

Turning Points (Jackson & Davis, 2000) recommended that middle schools organize learning climates that promote intellectual development and shared educational purpose. Moreover, they further recommended that effective middle schools provide a safe and healthy school environment. Collectively, the researchers in this book have shown how single-sex classes affected the academic achievement and the social development of young adolescents. Whether they are in the heartland of the United States or the heart of Africa, single-sex classes provide a compelling way to accommodate the educational needs of adolescents.

REFERENCES

American Association of University Women. (1998) *Separated by sex: A critical look at single-sex education for girls.* Washington, DC: AAUW.

Datnow, A., Hubbard, L., & Conchas, G. (2001). How context mediates policy: The implementation of single-sex public schooling in California. *Teacher's College Record, 103*(2), 184–206.

Dee, T. S. (2006). *The why chromosome: How a teacher's gender affects boys and girls.* (Hoover Institution, Education Next, 2006: No. 4). Stanford, CA: Stanford University.

Fennema, E., & Carpenter, T. (1981). Sex-related differences in mathematics: Results from national assessment. *The Mathematics Teacher, 74*, 554–559.

Gilson, J. (1999, April 19–23). *Single-sex education versus coeducation for girls: A study of mathematics achievement and attitudes toward mathematics of middle school students.* Paper presented at the Annual Meeting of the American Educational Research Association, Montreal.

Jackson, A., & Davis, G. (2000). *Turning points 2000: Educating adolescents in the 21st century.* New York: Teachers College Press.

Kleinfeld, J. (1999). Student performance: Males versus females. *The Public Interest, 134*, 3–20.

Krug, E. (1964). *The shaping of the American high school: 1880–1920.* Madison: University of Wisconsin Press.

Lee, V., & Bryk, A. (1986). Effects of single-sex secondary schools on student achievement and attitudes. *Journal of Educational Psychology, 78*, 381–395.

Mulholland, J., Hanson, P., & Kaminski, E. (2004). Do single-sex classrooms in coeducational settings address boys' underachievement? An Australian study. *Educational Studies, 30*(1), 19–32.

Sadker, M., & Sadker, D. (1994). *Failing at fairness: How our schools cheat girls.* New York: Touchstone.

Salomone, R. (2003). *Same, different, equal: Rethinking single-sex schooling.* New Haven, CT: Yale University Press.

Sax, L. (2005). *Why gender matters: What parents and teachers need to know about the emerging science of sex differences.* New York: Doubleday.

Steedman, J. (1985). Examination results in mixed and single-sex secondary schools. In D. Reynolds (Ed.), *Studying school effectiveness* (pp. 87–101). London: Falmer Press.

Tyack, D. & Hansot, E. (2002) Feminists discover the hidden injuries of coeducation. In E. Rassen, L. Iura, & P. Berkman (Eds.), *Gender in education* (pp. 12–50). San Francisco: Jossey-Bass.

Van de Gaer, E., Pustjens, H., Van Damme, J., & DeMunter, A. (2004). Effects of single-sex versus co-educational classes and schools on gender differences in progress in language and mathematics achievement. *British Journal of Sociology of Education, 25*(3), 307–323.

Vu, P. (2006, September 19). Single-gender schools on the rise. Stateline.org. Retrieved September 21, 2006, from www.stateline.org.

2

Jumping into the Fray

How to Implement Single-Sex Classes

Deborah E. Marks and C. Sloan Burns

It started with a scream. It started with a teacher suffering a panic attack. One of our best 6th-grade teachers ran into my office screaming, "You won't believe this, my class roll, it's all girls, all girls!" How was this possible? A little while later another teacher flew in and reported that her class roll was all boys. This made two teams out of five single sex, a computer fluke, and, as it turned out, serendipity. The second teacher was much calmer. She knew that this situation would naturally be rectified; certainly the administration would clean up this mess. Yet I was not so sure.

Something nagged at me, and over three days and three nights I spoke to numerous professionals in education. I spoke to colleagues and retired teachers, and I read research and articles. I tossed and turned through sleepless nights struggling over what to do. What was unintentionally created—what had been literally dropped in my lap—were two single-sex classes. Furthermore, these two classes (due to the fact that one was all male and one all female), just so happened to meet the letter of the law. We had released class rolls on the Monday of teacher workweek, the week before school opened. By Thursday of that week I had decided to keep them as they were. I committed us to take the plunge into comparatively unknown waters.

Typically, a decision like this takes years of research, planning, and communication. We all know that parental buy-in with a project like this is paramount. Even then, the logistical issues of a master schedule can gum up the works and postpone implementation a year or more. In our case, however, the schedule was in place. Light-speed research on the topic had convinced me that it was worth doing. Now, we only had to cram approximately two years of study, discussion, and ownership in by sometime before Tuesday—and Monday was a holiday. A year of teacher committee work and team-building exercises, a year of parental meetings and building ownership, all of this, and more, done in . . . what, two days? We were the accidental field test. Luckily our staff and parents already worked as a team.

Once I had decided to go forth with this, my first step was to calm the teachers. Teachers' reactions were varied. During the first week of school, letters were sent out to parents to inform them that their children were enrolled in single-gender teams. In the letter, parents were informed that they could withdraw their children from the program. However, we purposely waited five days to send the letter. Amazingly, during that waiting period no one mentioned to any of the students or the parents that their classes were single gender. I suspect that the students really didn't notice; it is good to gain an appreciation of the 6th-grade mind. Nothing was mentioned at our back-to-school night either. No, we waited a week so that the students would bond with their teachers, classmates, and schedule. It wasn't until then that we informed the parents.

As a result, none of the parents requested to remove their children from the program. I did get a couple of calls from parents asking why I waited so long to notify them. In my case, I had the perfect excuse. And before you get carried away, please remember that since this all happened due to a scheduling fluke, permission was never requested. My advice is to gain permission before committing. Shortly after our letter was sent home, the buzz started at the local grocery stores. Soon parents were calling with questions and requests to come in and observe. Parents also called requesting that their children be enrolled in one of the teams. What we discovered with these requests was that the students really were in charge. The parents may have wanted their children to be enrolled in the program but if a child wasn't interested, it didn't happen. The bottom line is that none of the kids wanted to change. Those who were in the single-gender classes loved it and didn't want out. Those who were in the traditional classes didn't want in.

We later discovered that this option was particularly useful as an opportunity for students who were experiencing difficulties in the regular setting, with issues that ranged from low grades, bullying, and behavior that might often lead parents to seek alternative placement. We had an alternative placement ready for them in-house.

Realizing that single-sex classes are anything but the latest thing, I was in a quandary on how to proceed. Basically, I was looking at reintroducing 18th-century educational policy. How would I dress up yesteryear's has-been in 21st-century clothes? How would I make single-sex classes sing, especially in the present-day cold-feet environment? Public school education isn't exactly famous for risk taking. Worst of all, how would I endear this idea to all concerned when we got our project timeline backward?

We had to get across the point that the single-sex grouping is a plus. We had to communicate that placement in single-sex classes would allow students to blossom and grow. Single-sex classes would remove distractions that often hinder a student's personal and intellectual maturation. Parents and teachers needed to know that single-sex classes were good for their kids, and they needed to know right away. Luckily the kids were happy and doing well, so most of our work was done for us. So the parents were essentially sold before we had a chance to sell them.

IF WE HAD DONE THIS THE RIGHT WAY

If I had to do it over again, if there hadn't been a computer fluke, if those teachers had never complained to me, I would never have done this. Let it be known that this was my first year as principal of this middle school and single-gender education was the last thing on my mind. Suddenly, after my crash course in the subject, it made perfect sense to me to introduce this to 6th-grade classes. Do I really need to describe the workings of the middle school mind? Let's just say that the transition from elementary to middle school is dramatic. The choice of words here is not accidental. Middle school is all about drama. There is drama for the staff, drama for the students, and drama for the parents. If we can provide one less thing to worry about, everyone is thankful. Thankfulness is often quite rare in public school, and I was itching for some.

If we had planned to introduce single-gender classes to our school we would have started two years ago. Let me take that back: maybe three years ago. I probably would have studied it myself for at least a few months, maybe a year. So let's assume that after a few months of study, I was convinced that this is the way to go. Two years before implementation, I would build ownership with our staff. I would invite professionals in to train the staff on single-gender classes, communicating to them the benefits, especially for the age group. We would bring in a facilitator to meet with our 6th-grade teachers during their team-planning periods over a good amount of time. I would want this third-party facilitator to get to know the teachers well. The facilitator would engage the teachers in activities designed to develop instructional techniques specific to single-gender classes. During these activities the facilitator would gain appreciation for each teacher's strengths and growth areas. In turn, this valuable information would be used by the administration for teacher assignment.

So, two years before our first student was to enroll, we would have built our teams of teachers. Teacher selection would have taken quite a bit of time too. As you may be aware, teachers make or break an initiative; ultimately they drive your school. Therefore, we would have had to find the best match for the four core areas. It was our English, math, social studies, and science classes that were to be single gender. These are, by the way, also the classes affected by our state's standards-based high-stakes testing program during certain benchmark years. These students would reach the next assessment in the 8th-grade. Therefore, teacher selection was crucial. Not only would we want to select the best teacher for our 6th-grade math class, but that person would also have to be the best for our 6th-grade math class *of all girls*. Then we would need to decide who would be the best to teach a 6th-grade class of all boys.

Meanwhile, our team members would have been involved in extensive staff development. Our faculty would need to know what they were going to be doing, so they would have spent time researching single-gender classes on paper and in person. Arrangements would have been made for them to observe any single-gender classes we could find within driving distance.

A year before implementation, our teachers would be assigned and ready. We would then arrange to meet with the administration of our feeder schools. These meetings would communicate our mission and the justification and logistics of the plan. We would need buy-in from the staff of all of our feeder schools. Actually, we would want more than buy-in: We would want to empower the feeder school staff to sell and communicate the program. They would need to be informed well enough to answer all the questions they would get. All of this would be in preparation for a January elementary school PTA meeting. With the collective staff of our middle school and the elementary schools we could do a nice job of communication and building excitement. In hindsight, building excitement wouldn't have been hard; if nothing else, this is exciting work.

During March, once schedules were done, we would have had a Meet-the-Teachers Night. During this event we would have held information sessions on our single-gender program for our parents. We would have flooded them with opportunities to learn. Parents would have become aware that at any time in the spring or summer they could call to enroll their children in the program. They would also be aware that they could withdraw their children from the program at any time. Then, at last, we would be ready to send out the schedule request forms for the next year and play the waiting game before we knew how many students would select the single-gender teams.

Meanwhile staff development and planning would be ongoing with our two teams of teachers. Time—including professional leave time—would have to be set aside to do a great deal of team building. This kind of work cannot be completed during planning periods and after-school meetings. Team building does not stop with our staff; the students would need to come together. We could start with summer events, such as picnics with the teams of students and their teachers. These activities are helpful in the transition from elementary to middle school. Plus, with a number of these events, students', parents', and even teachers' fears could be addressed and soothed.

It must be understood that staff development is a continuous activity due to the fact that research on single-gender education is constantly being updated. When I was confronted with this opportunity in 2002 there were fewer than 50 known schools that were using single-gender grouping in a way to enhance student success in a public school setting.

Faced with little time and zero knowledge base, I began my research to find out where these schools were and, if possible, make arrangements to visit them. We felt that we needed to gather as much practical information as we could get as quickly as possible. That began the teachers' process of learning more and more about single-gender classes. They had been thrown into teaching all girls or all boys with no experience or knowledge. They were thrown in blind, and what we found is that they were doing a great job at it. Due to their enthusiasm, dedication, and creative thinking, they were doing as good a job with these groups as many multiple-year veterans do. Knowledge of their successes validated their efforts and, in turn, invigorated them. Boy, were they pumped.

Next the newspapers started calling. Word had gotten out to the press about what we were doing. Subsequently articles began to appear in a number of local papers. We got calls from the local television stations, also. The next thing we knew, we were appearing on the local evening news, on all three stations. Then the big call came: A representative from *The News Hour with Jim Lehrer* called to make arrangements to send an advance team to interview parents, students, and staff. They were to interview to gather viewpoints on our single-gender classes that sprang up overnight. We were so fired up about this opportunity that it took relatively little effort to organize the schedule for these interviews. Next, arrangements were made for Mr. Lehrer's visit, and our folks were prepared and organized for a full day of filming and interviewing for a show that was to be aired in the near future on PBS.

Prior to the following year we began our work in organizing the continuation of this initiative. With all of this great press, we were overwhelmed with requests to enroll in the program. We arranged for numerous meetings with parents, and before the school year ended we had already signed up two full teams of girls. We also had a team of boys. We surveyed our parents to discover why we had fewer boys. What we found was that the boys were concerned about their sexual orientation coming into question. Basically, they were afraid of being called "gay" for being in the all-boys team, conveniently ignoring the fact that they all sign up for shop class together. After the first year, of the 100-plus girls of the all-girls team, 75 decided to stay in the all-girls team for the 7th grade. Another 15 from the traditional classes joined the 75 in the 7th grade. The boys were another story. Out of the 100 on the original all-boys team, only 15 decided to stay for the next year. We made one section on a team for those 15.

The decrease in the number of boys the following year probably could have been avoided if there had been greater commitment from the teachers on the all-boys team. If we had provided that team of teachers more support in training and activities, we may have had a completely different outcome. In retrospect, I should have anticipated the problem. Now, I don't have any empirical evidence to support this, but I knew that our teachers were used to getting positive feedback from girls and not so much from boys. Therefore, we should have allocated greater resources in team building for the all-boys team. The fact that the all-boys team failed nicely underscores the importance of adequate staff development. I cannot emphasize enough the necessity of thorough, long-term staff development. The experience certainly solidified my outlook on teacher training: Real staff development, that which makes a lasting difference in instruction, must be meaningful, thorough, and long term.

Options for this kind of training are slim. The bottom line is that your teachers are going to need real classes in how boys and girls learn differently, and how to adjust curriculum and instruction to meet the different needs. We would do well by having our local universities and colleges offer such classes. A two-week full-time, full-day course would be minimal and could work well within the constraints of our school calendars.

COMMUNITY INVOLVEMENT

As mentioned above, we informed the parents of the single-gender classes after school had begun. With time on our side, we would have handled things very differently. We would have informed our community long before and allowed students to sign up for these teams. As it turned out, however, none of our students opted to leave the first year, and we had other families that wanted to enroll. Even with minimal time to build community involvement, we enjoyed a great deal of excitement. A parent was quoted on the PBS spot, saying, "This is the best of both worlds; it's like having our own private school."

Successes included the fact that we had more honor roll students from these teams than the rest of the school. We had far fewer discipline referrals from the single-gender teams, and attendance was far greater. So, as the data revealed, three important results in our experience with single-gender grouping were exposed: better grades, better attendance, and better behavior. These successes continued with the all-girls team for the following 3 years. Beyond the academics, the girls experienced success and community service outside the classroom. Over the course of the 3 years, the all-girls team was involved in service learning. Plus, through these activities the girls were exposed to women who were successful in a variety of careers. Essentially, the young women left our program empowered with the idea that they could be successful in any field they chose. Furthermore, the parents of these girls were really our best spokespeople. Their impact on the community was far greater than we could ever have hoped for. In both formal and informal contexts, these parents passionately sang the praises of our school and program. We can give these folks a great deal of credit for the growth and success of our school.

The successes in our program were shared with all of our stakeholders in March, including PTAs from our feeder schools as well as other members of the community. In order to fulfill their goal of a 100-member class, the all-girls team teachers engaged in a recruitment campaign. To illustrate their commitment to the program, they spent their summer calling students and parents to get the numbers they wanted. The 6th-grade team did not have any recruitment problems: quite the contrary. News of the successes of our single-gender classes had spread across our feeder elementary schools. The popularity of our program was such that we found that we had to turn some away from our 6th-grade all-girls team.

As the third year approached the media hype had calmed down. Now the program had become institutionalized; the single-gender program was simply a fact for our school. During our third year, we were busy selecting staff for our 8th-grade teams and promoting the program through our elementary school outreach activities. We had been so successful through outreach that not only did we have a full team of females, but we also had 50 males. In the middle of spreading the word, I received a call from a parent who had heard about our single-gender classes from her elementary school. She was incensed with what we were doing; she threatened to alert the media and called me a "bra-burning lesbian." She added that it was clear to her that all I was doing was promoting homosexuality through these classes. So not everyone was happy. However, on the bright side, you know that you're making a positive difference when the crazy people start calling you up.

During the 3 years I read every piece of literature I could find on single-gender classes. I frequented conferences, visited like schools, and was eventually named as a member of the national board for the National Association for Single Sex Public Education. What I discovered was that the pool of information and number of schools experimenting with this form of education was growing. When I first started looking into this topic in 2002, I found about a dozen schools; now there are more than 200.

I guess all of you are wondering whether this was and is worth it. Was it worth the sleepless nights, the confusion, and the angry calls? I am at a new school now and I have had time to reflect on the middle school experience. When the computer fluke was found and I had processed and read the research, I knew that this was good for students. I think I did the right thing and gave people a choice. Sure, I would do things differently if I were to implement this in another school. But I would definitely offer the opportunity to all of our children. We are proud of our successes and we are proud that we have made a difference for our young men and our young women. Our experience has made a difference beyond the walls of this middle school. A neighboring middle school found inspiration to investigate and research single-gender grouping from their observations of our experience. They began their own single-gender program in 2003.

3

Bumps Along the Way
Mistakes Made and Lessons Learned

Suzanne Schwarz-McCotter

"How do you feel about single-gender classrooms?" This was the question posed to teachers and administrators of Rogers Middle School[1] in the summer of 2003. Rogers Middle School is a socioeconomically and ethnically diverse Title I middle school in a small urban area of southern Pennsylvania. The district's population is highly transient, and 75% of Rogers's students live below the poverty line. Single-gender classes were one of many strategies implemented by leaders to solve some of the problems facing the school.

The complex results of the attempt are difficult to characterize as simply a success or a failure. Rather, they illustrate the impact of leadership, both formal and informal, at different levels of education. From the risk-taking modeled by the superintendent to the social hierarchy of the students, both successes and failures can be linked to absence or evidence of leadership qualities.

THE CONTEXT

Walking through the halls of Rogers today, outsiders would be hard-pressed to know how far the school has come. Between 2000 and 2002, the school was led by four principals. Plagued by poor media reports and a worse reputation, the public perception was of a deteriorating and dangerous facility, unruly and out-of-control students, and battle-scarred and burnt-out teachers.[2] Spring 2002 brought a dramatic shift to the school's climate when the associate superintendent stepped in as acting principal for several months, bringing along a highly effective assistant principal. Within weeks, both students and teachers heaved a collective sigh of relief as it became clear that a competent and caring leader had taken the first steps to turning the school's climate around.

A new permanent principal was brought in to continue the school's revitalization, the assistant principal provided consistency through the transition, and the associate superintendent became the district's superintendent. With effective leadership in the school's corner, Rogers was poised to begin focusing on student learning. For several years, test scores had illuminated the impact of the school's struggles on student achievement. The most recent, more successful year had show increases in assessment data, but not at sufficient levels to be considered adequate yearly progress (AYP). As the superintendent and school administrators brainstormed about possible solutions, the idea of single-gender classrooms emerged.

The logistics were left in the hands of the school administrators, who determined the details such as teacher recruitment, student assignment, and parent notification. Since 6th- and 7th-grade classes were already organized into dyads (teams of 2 teachers and 50 to 60 students), it was determined that one dyad at each grade would be designated as single gender. Students in the school were also grouped by achievement level, based primarily on reading scores and supplemented by teacher recommendation. Both of the targeted dyads were composed of students in "Express" classes, the designation used for below-standard groups. Encouraged by the superintendent to also try the single-gender grouping with academically on-standard students, the trial was also extended to two of the four classes on an 8th-grade team after the first several months of school.

Selecting the right teachers for the single-gender classes was an important decision for the school leaders. The assistant principal described the criteria used to select teachers: "We looked for teachers who . . . were interested in doing it, and . . . teachers that were better at building relationships with kids. Not necessarily being friendly with kids, but just building that relationship and that consistency." Without benefit of knowing how administrators made their decisions, teachers made some assumptions about their selection. One teacher, reflecting on why the principal had selected her and her dyad partner as teachers of single-gender classes, said,

[My teaching partner] and I complement each other as teachers very well. We're both solid planners. [He's] much firmer outwardly with his discipline . . . and mine is a much more backdoor approach. . . . So in that way it's a good complement. Personally and professionally, I thought it was really neat to have the opportunity. I think he must think I'm a pretty good teacher, which made me feel really good.

Although she was uncomfortable saying that she recognized the compliment behind her selection, this teacher recognized the implied praise for her practice.

After selecting the teachers, administrators assigned students to the single-gender sections. Students had already been designated onto teams or dyads, and they were not changed once the decision to group by gender was made. The school leaders assigned the girls to one homeroom teacher and the boys to another, and designed schedules so that the groups would move through all of their core academic classes together. Although parents were given the chance to opt out on behalf of their children, none did.

"WE'LL GIVE IT A SHOT"

As unyielding to change as typical school cultures can be, any innovation carries the greatest chance of success when accompanied by teacher buy-in and professional development. This has been established in connection with technology (Watson, 2006), block scheduling (Meister & Nolan, 2001), and curriculum shifts (Frykholm, 2005), and is certainly true about beginning to teach students in configurations as different as single-gender groups.

Effective professional development has key aspects of both process and substance (Clark et al., 1996; Darling-Hammond & McLaughlin, 1996; Lieberman, 1995; Little, 1993; McCotter, 2001). Process elements include teacher input, sustained commitment over time, foundation in local needs, and collaboration. Substantive elements include specific learning goals and a connection to student learning.

Leaders at Rogers Middle School and from the district had good intentions for professional development when they initiated single-gender classes, as the assistant principal described:

We went into this with a plan that we would start this and then with "x" amount of dollars that would be coming because we were doing it, we would be able to seek out and find professional development and/or research . . . using this money to work with the teachers that are doing it so that they could get . . . professional development.

The end of that story is all too predictable, as it often is in low-achieving, high-poverty districts: "But there was no money." The teachers told the same story: "[T]he superintendent . . . had said that there was extra grant money available which never came to pass. . . . Halfway through the year, it was frustrating to hear, but we [just said] 'Whatever, . . . we'll give it a shot.'"

It appears then, that although the formal professional development never materialized, some aspects of effective professional development actually did exist. The teachers had input to the process, including their personal agreement to participate in the single-gender initiative. They saw themselves as collaborators with the administrators and with one another in their work. The endeavor and teacher growth were clearly grounded in the local context and needs.

The keys that were missing in terms of professional development were substantive, and it was both disappointing to all involved and a piece that may have made all the difference for sustained success. Yet another change in district leadership[3] led to a new superintendent, which may have contributed to the absence of support for professional development. One administrator said,

> We needed to work with professional development . . . with the teachers. We were seeking some outlets, finding folks that could come in and work with us on this. But then [the new superintendent] came in and we brought it up, and said, "This is something we're working with, the teachers are doing a good job with it, but they need training, they need resources, they need ideas." . . . But there was no money, there was no push from board level, from superintendent level saying that we want to continue this, there was no financial incentive for doing it.

In the absence of sustained commitment and a knowledge base for their practice, teachers relied on their own instincts and best practices for working with the students.

Along with the normal reflection[4] that goes with trying different instructional strategies until finding ones that are effective, the teachers' personal professional development took three avenues. The first was relying on their immediate professional community. The teams of teachers who worked with single-gender classes depended on each other for support and new ideas. The second strategy was to reach out to the broader professional community. Teachers read and shared books about gender by Sadker and Sadker (1994) and Pollack (1998) in an effort to attain greater understanding.

The third professional development strategy used by the teachers was a unique and innovative one. Three of the teachers who taught single-gender classes also served as cooperating teachers to postbaccalaureate interns from a local university.[5] Along with instructional responsibilities, these interns also had academic requirements to develop field-based case studies, complete action research, and perform service to the school. The teachers and interns worked together on these assignments so that they would both be useful to the practical needs of teaching single-gender classes and meet the academic needs of the interns. Outcomes of these efforts included case studies on behavior in single-gender classes, a resource book of articles and strategies to use in single-gender classrooms, and a comparative analysis of final grades in core subjects.

This collaborative effort on the part of teachers and interns certainly drew from aspects of using both the local and greater professional community, but it also added an additional level of outcome to the efforts. Because interns were responsible for creating formal products, the research led to a different result than would have been otherwise possible given the time constraints of most teachers. The added benefit to the interns was seeing the need and audience served by their academic work, bringing an increased level of authenticity to an academic exercise.

The commitment of professionals to learning how to be the best possible teachers for their students, and the lack of resources to formally support their learning, paints a picture of two kinds of leadership. Those who worked most closely with students saw the need to learn how to effectively teach in single-gender settings. Both the administrators and the teachers who were in daily contact with students identified the need for professional development and took steps to achieve it. The teachers not only put forth great effort to learn about gender and learning, but also modeled professional commitment to the novice teachers who were working with them. The lack of leadership from the district, on the other hand, was disappointing to everyone at Rogers Middle School. Funds promised, but never committed, led to a perceived lack of support for the school, teachers, and students.

"NOBODY MESSES WITH ZASHA"

The implications of strong leadership among adults had a clear impact on the teachers of single-gender classes at Rogers. However, there was a striking corollary in the impact of student leadership. When both teachers and administrators discussed and described the social aspects of single-gender classes, they specifically focused on the role of social hierarchies among students and the differences in those hierarchies in all-girls and all-boys classes.

This aspect first became clear in the work of the postbaccalaureate in-terns, who did individual case studies of students in their classes. Two sep-arate cases that focused on girls from the single-gender 7th-grade class mentioned the relationship of the subject to another girl in the class—Zasha. Inquiry into this coincidence revealed that not only was Zasha the absolute leader in this group, but that interns in the other single-gender classrooms had also observed similar phenomena. The school's assistant principal confirmed the observations: "[T]he classes were successful if that person, that Alpha wolf or whatever you want to call them, had the right mindset."

Zasha was mentioned by name by each educator who worked with the 7th-grade classes, and her influence was both positive and dynamic. One administrator described her influence:

> Nobody messes with her. Her primary focus in school was learning, doing schoolwork. She was a good student, but you didn't mess with her. . . . She was at the top of that pecking order, and that attitude permeated down through the rest of the girls. "OK, we're here to learn, we're here to get along, stop disrupting my class and acting like a fool." And, if Zasha said it, that's how it was.

One of her teachers reflected on Zasha's own growth, as well as her lead-ership of the class: "Zasha's growth didn't come academically. It came socially for her. . . . She led the classroom. Where Zasha went, the other girls went too. No one really challenged her."

The all-girls 7th-grade class established a definite culture throughout the year, and several adults give credit to Zasha's leadership. The grade leader with responsibility for discipline described their community norms:

> But by the end of that year that core group of girls was a unit upon themselves. You know they didn't get into middle school "he-said/she-said" stuff. They had almost like a protocol, "this is how we do things in our class." We sit down, we talk it out . . . it was interesting. And I really saw it . . . when there were problems because the two who had their problem, not all of them, . . . would come to the office saying ,"[W]e need to talk this out. There's a problem, people are saying things, and we need to work this out." And I can't say that happens other places. And maybe it does, . . . but not with the frequency that it goes on in that class.

Although it would be hard to isolate one causal factor for the community, adults generously gave Zasha credit.

Leadership in some of the other classes had different effects. The all-girls 8th-grade class ended up having an adversarial relationship with several of their teachers. A cycle started where the teachers began to be engaged in escalating conflicts with the girls' class. An administrator described it:

> The girls' class would challenge the authority more often and that's what they [the teachers] found difficult. . . . There was the whole issue about standing for the pledge . . . that came out of that girls' class. There was some very social, . . . "let's buck the system whatever the system is we don't care" kind of thing. So they would look for things where they could push. They knew they didn't have to stand for the pledge, they ran with that because they knew they would win. And that became one of those areas that were a little sore for some . . . because the girls were right, they knew they didn't have to, some of us wanted to make an issue out of it and they lost. Can't make them stand for the pledge.

In this case, it was not an individual student who served as the social leader of the class, but a collective goal to resist leadership by the teachers.

Teachers and administrators described a "pecking order" in the all-boys classes based on a variety of social issues, including racial identity, athletic ability, and who was friends with whom. The interns from the post-baccalaureate program suggested that, from their perspective, a few 8th-grade boys were competing with their male teachers to be the class leader. This led to serious resistance to learning, or doing any work expected by those teachers. Because of scheduling constraints, the 8th-grade classes did not become separated by gender until after the first marking period, allowing a comparison of individuals' grades in both mixed- and single-gender classes. In every core subject, the percentage of 8th-grade boys passing the class *decreased* once they were in all-boys sections.

There were also social implications for the boys' classes. The assistant principal said:

> Some guys that weren't real serious, that were the top of the pecking order, serious about getting an education, and that attitude then permeated, or became their identity. There was a whole maturity piece, and that's why the social benefit for the girls was so much easier. The boys, it took a lot of work. . . . They were too immature, and they were too mistrusting of each other. They were too unwilling to work together as a group of students. I can't say all middle school boys are like that, but this group was.

Ironically, trying to protect the single-gender classes from changing population throughout the year may have exacerbated the problem. In a school that has "tremendous turnover" throughout the year, most teachers find that their roster changes drastically from one month to the next as students enroll and withdraw. One administrator said that the "pecking order" problem may have been clearer in single-gender classes because the school leadership tried to maintain "purity" of the classes and did not add new students to their classes as frequently as they did to mixed-gender classes. This gave the single-gender classes an opportunity to identify and sustain a clearer pecking order than the mixed-gender classes where there was a "constant change that affects that pecking order."

It is worth noting that the 6th-grade teachers did not comment on the "pecking order" to the same extent as the 7th- and 8th-grade teachers. Educators will not be surprised that the social interaction of early adolescents plays an important role in the decisions they make and that the role of peers increases as adolescence approaches. Knowing this, however, does not detract from the striking point made by the illustrations of student leadership in single-gender classrooms.

"I WAS AN HONORARY BOY"

Before starting their work with single-gender groups, both teachers and administrators had some preconceptions about how that work would differ from working with mixed-gender classes. A male administrator described the suppositions he had held:

> [I always said,] "Oh, give me a classroom with boys, no problem, we'll always be OK." We had one teacher saying that's how he felt, [but] it was such a shock and an eye-opener to have a class of 20-something girls, and when you said something like you would say to a group of boys, the girls get upset, and you [had to talk about it]! I grew up in a . . . you punch each other in the arm, you get past it, you move on, but no, it wasn't that easy.

It was important for both the administrators and teachers to acknowledge the preconceptions they had held and to recognize how the reality either confirmed or challenged these preconceptions. The same male administrator said this was an important issue that could have been addressed if they'd had more support for professional development: "We should have spent time with our teachers on that. . . . I think we went into it a little bit blind, and we should have spent more time really looking at it."

The female teacher of 6th-graders had attempted to prepare for her role as a teacher of single-gender classes over the summer by reading professional literature.[6] She found herself surprised, however, by the reality:

> [T]he first time you get a room full of all boys, and not ever having been a boy, it was a good three weeks of just learning how they relate to each other. . . . [A]nd I read over the summer, you know, "Boys think differently and girls think differently," and I had the book and read the book and I thought I was ready, until they walked in the door. And then the farting started and then the busting, the ripping on each other, just mean. You know, girls at least, aren't outwardly mean. Not saying we're not mean. We just don't tend to do it like that, in your face.

Her attempt to become academically prepared for the challenges that faced her was quickly mediated by the reality of a classroom full of preadolescent boys.

It is a testament to many of the teachers in this school that they persevered to gain a greater understanding of how to work with single-gender groups by listening to and observing their students, and modifying professional practices to meet student needs. The same 6th-grade teacher described when she finally had a breakthrough with her male students:

> I remember we had our first honest conversation in the boys' class . . . because they don't talk about their feelings that much. But . . . once they became comfortable with each other, they shared a lot of things. I realized that the whole misconception that boys don't feel things is completely wrong. It was interesting to see how their feelings got hurt a lot more easily over things I thought were silly, [like getting called last for lunch every day]. . . . And it wasn't just one, four or five of them were convinced that [the lunch monitor] didn't like them. OK, so I listened, and that was the strange thing, to realize that they needed assurance, but they weren't going to trust—and that's what it was. That's what the change was. They realized that they could trust me enough to tell me their feelings. When that happened, the room changed. . . . There were two or three leaders in that group, the boys' group, that ran the classroom, and when they got comfortable enough to know that I wasn't going to trash them or their feelings, those kinds of conversations happened. I began to feel more like, even though I had a set of breasts, I was an honorary boy.

This teacher experienced a significant moment of understanding about her male students by listening carefully to their needs—and responding to them. Her recognition led to the ability to make greater strides in instruction, as the boys became more willing to have in-depth conversations about theoretical concepts in social studies and take greater risks in their writing.

A hallmark of good teaching includes the ability to reflect on one's practice and make changes based on input from others (including colleagues and students). Higher levels of reflection are characterized by a focus on student learning, the ability to generalize changes to one's teaching approach, and asking ongoing questions about one's practice (Ward & McCotter, 2004). This teacher's description of her teaching practice is an example of how the effective teachers in the single-gender settings were able to take advantage of new situations that challenged their preconceptions in order to model effective teaching.

"WE FAILED SO MANY OF THEM"

Working in this new setting without additional support structures in place proved exhausting for the teachers. Not only did they not receive the extra resources they felt they had been promised, but they also were disappointed by what they perceived as their failures. As an example, a 7th-grade teacher described the academic outcome of the all-boys class:

> [My teaching partner] and I were burnt out from the lack of academic success with the boys' class. The girls were more academically successful. We had about 5 failures, 5 kids we retained in 7th grade for the year. And . . . they were all from the boys' class. And it was upsetting to us because, well, we both take it personally, we couldn't let it go, you know?

For hardworking teachers who pride themselves in effecting student learning, 5 retentions out of 50 students was too high, and they saw their lack of experience in teaching single-gender classes as a contributing factor.

These teachers, after collaborative conversations with the building administrators, decided to keep the all-girls class intact for a second year.[7] The structure of the team changed from a two-teacher 7th-grade team to a four-teacher 8th-grade team. The single-gender class of girls looped with their 7th-grade teachers and also had two additional teachers for their 8th-grade year. The other three classes on the team were mixed gender.

The group of girls in their second year continued to grow, both socially and academically. This was true even though they had lost their leader, Zasha, when she was moved to a more academically advanced class. An indicator of the closeness of their community came at the end of the year, when the transition to high school was looming. A teacher noted this: "Change is hard for them. They've been fighting the fact that they're leaving since mid-May. We started graduation practice and their behavior problems started. They started acting up, they started getting sent out."

This was a departure from their typical actions, and the teacher and postbaccalaureate intern (Annie) in the class tried to use their weekly classroom meetings to figure out what was happening in the community. A particular concern was that although some new students had been added to the class during the year, the students who were getting in trouble were the ones who had met with so much success in their 2 years in the all-girls class. Students were unusually reticent about the possible causes until close to the end of the year, as the teacher recounted:

> It wasn't until Annie left. Annie left the last week in May and we had a meeting that day instead of Friday. And we had a circle, and it was a huge fight. Two girls who have been friends since 3rd grade weren't talking to each other. Pretending the other didn't exist. And, we have a pregnant girl, and she started to cry. And when she started to cry, about 4 or 5 others did too, and Jessica actually said, "I feel like my life is changing. I feel like nothing's ever going to be the same." And that was it. I'm done, I'm bawling, and Annie's bawling, so that's what it is. Once Jessie admitted it, it was OK, because the rest of them could too. And that's heartbreaking to let them go like that. I don't know what they're gonna face academically.

The transition from single gender to mixed gender was an emotional one for everyone at this level. With the all-girls class, which had grown to such a great extent, the transition was fear of what would come next. With the all-boys class, the emotion was regret. Both teachers felt that they had let the boys down, as one teacher expressed: "I walked away feeling like it was academically a failure. But I don't know if there's another way to look at it. We failed so many of them."

"I STILL THINK GOOD THINGS CAME OUT OF IT"

The initiative to implement single-gender classrooms at Rogers Middle School cannot be portrayed as successful. There was no objective evidence that students were more successful academically, and the social benefits were mixed. Teachers who had been identified as effective by their selection for the single-gender classes felt as though they had not been successful. The initiative itself was not sustained beyond the first year in most cases.

There were, however, some individual glimpses of success in the initiative that can be attributed to the circumstances set up by this initiative. The female teacher of 7th graders (who became an "honorary boy") found her voice as a teacher leader during this year. Being asked to participate in this initiative by the school leaders let her know that they respected her teaching ability, and she gained confidence that had not previously existed. It was her determination that kept the all-girls class going during the second year, and she has since begun a master's degree in educational leadership and become a schoolwide instructional facilitator.

The community of 7th-grade girls that was sustained for a second year became a cohesive group in the school. Each adult who was interviewed recognized that group as unique because of the way they bonded and worked with and for one another. Their articulation at the end of the year that they were afraid of what was going to happen next is an unusual expression for a class of 8th graders and is a testament to the teachers' ability to facilitate a sense of community.

Zasha stands out as an important symbol for that community. She was able to use her strong presence as a leader in the all-girls group to help the focus of the class become academic. Her personal success allowed her to move to a group with higher achievement levels in 8th grade. Although she was no longer part of the tight-knit girls' group, she visited frequently. She is now part of an academically oriented small learning community in high school, and seems to be sustaining the work habits and leadership she attained in her year as "leader of the girls."

With more district support, professional development, and material resources, the benefits of this initiative may have been greater or more tangible, but the glimmers of success were important to the individuals who were affected. The school principal summed up his thoughts about the initiative in this way: "I still think good things came out of it, without a doubt, because there were good teachers teaching the kids, and whether they're all boys, all girls, whatever, that didn't matter."

NOTES

1. All proper names are pseudonyms.
2. See McCotter (2002) for more details, as well as a description of the author's role in the school.

3. A sad postscript to this leader's story is that his success as a building leader was not sustained in district leadership, and he was forced to resign from his position as superintendent. It is possible that the subsequent lack of support from the district was the desire to end affiliation with a project that had been closely identified with the former superintendent.

4. Reflection is defined as inquiry about teaching practices tied to purposive action (see Ward & McCotter, 2004).

5. These interns were adults with bachelor's degrees who had come back to college to pursue teaching certification. They worked with a cooperating teacher over the course of an academic year in a field-based program coordinated and supervised by the author.

6. The teacher could not remember the book she had read over the summer, but her description of it suggests *Real Boys*.

7. This was the only group that maintained a single-gender model for the second year. The 8th-grade teachers became 7th-grade teachers and did not take single-gender classes. One of the 6th-grade teachers left, and the second could not find a partner willing to take single-gender classes on the team.

REFERENCES

Clark, C., Moss, P. A., Goering, S., Herter, R. J., Lamar, B., Leonard, D., Robbins, S., Russell, M., Templin, M., & Wascha, K. (1996). Collaboration as dialogue: Teachers and researchers engaged in conversation and professional development. *American Educational Research Journal, 33*(2), 193–231.

Darling-Hammond, L., & McLaughlin, M. W. (1996). Policies that support professional development in an era of reform. In M. W. McLaughlin & I. Oberman (Eds.), *Teacher learning: New policies, new practices* (pp. 202–218). New York: Teachers College Press.

Frykholm, J. (2005, Winter). Innovative curricula: Catalysts for reform in mathematics teacher education. *Action in Teacher Education, 26*(4), 20–36.

Lieberman, A. (1995). Practices that support teacher development. *Phi Delta Kappan, 76*(8), 591–596.

Little, J. W. (1993). Teachers' professional development in a climate of educational reform. *Educational Evaluation and Policy Analysis, 15*(2), 129–151.

McCotter, S. S. (2001). Collaborative groups as professional development. *Teaching and Teacher Education, 17*(6), 685–704.

McCotter, S. S. (2002, December). "If we only had better students": Re-learning how to be a good teacher. *Teaching Education, 13*(3), 329–340.

Meister, D, & Nolan, J. (2001, August). Out on a limb on our own: Uncertainty and doubt moving from subject-centered to interdisciplinary teaching. *Teachers College Record, 103*(4), 608–633.

Pollack, W. (1998). *Real boys: Rescuing our sons from the myths of boyhood.* New York: Random House.

Sadker, M., & Sadker, D. (1994). *Failing at fairness: How our schools cheat girls.* New York: Touchstone.

Ward, J. R. & McCotter, S. S. (2004). Reflection as a visible outcome for preservice teachers. *Teaching and Teacher Education, 20*(3), 243–257.

Watson, G. (2006, January). Technology professional development: Long-term effects on teacher self-efficacy. *Journal of Technology and Teacher Education, 14*(1), 151–166.

4

Having It Our Way

Students Speak Out on Single-Sex Classes

Frances R. Spielhagen

"**H**ave you ever heard of that saying, 'Time flies when you're having fun?' All-boy classes are fun!" James, age 11 and in the 6th grade, cheerfully offered his opinion of the single-gender academic classes at his public middle school. However, he quickly and quietly added a cautionary note, "Please write down that I will probably want to be with girls when I am in high school."

With equal enthusiasm, Melissa, age 13 and in the 8th grade, responded from her more adolescent point of view, "You can say what you want and not be afraid of being teased in all-girl classes . . . but sometimes we just want to be with the guys." Despite her satisfaction with the academic benefits of the single-gender arrangement, she clearly reinforced the developmental need of the adolescent for social interaction in mixed-gender environments. These divergent statements captured the essence of the student view of single-gender classes, a somewhat controversial paradigm that has gained popularity in public schools over the last few years.

Two key issues emerge when questioning students about single-gender classes. First, single-gender class arrangements seem to be most effective when related to the developmental needs of the students: The younger the student, the more likely that being in a single-gender class will be a positive experience. Second, in a public school environment, single-gender classes should presented as optional to parents and students, with flexibility within the school day and over the students' middle school years. These conclusions come through loud and clear when interviewing students who have experienced single-gender classes in their own public school.

THE CONTEXT OF INNOVATION

Since the fall of 2002, Forest Valley Middle School (a pseudonym), a public middle school of average size (N = 600 students) in rural New York State has provided a somewhat unique organizational arrangement that involves single-gender classes. The district has offered voluntary single-gender classes to all students in grades 6, 7, and 8 in four academic subjects: language arts, math, science, and social studies. All students in those grades remain in mixed-gender groups for all nonacademic classes and at lunchtime. Therefore, the students are not completely isolated from the peers of the opposite gender, but have time within the normal school day to interact and socialize. In the first year of the reform, approximately 75% of the students chose the single-gender academic classes. Over the last 2 years, the majority of those students have continued in single-gender classes.

The critical component of this arrangement was the element of choice within the routine structure of an established middle school with minimal disruption for the students. Because students were in single-gender classes in only the four academic areas, they interacted in mixed groups in all other classes, during lunch, and at other nonacademic experiences. The teachers who taught both single-gender and mixed classes attested to the cognitive benefits of the single-gender arrangement for those students who had selected that option. Parents also corroborated the teachers' perspectives, but it was the students themselves who offered the most salient observations of this phenomenon, which is regarded as new among public schools but actually has had a long history in American education.

HOW DID WE GET HERE?

Coeducation became a staple of American education in the Progressive Era of the early 20th century. Prior to the early 20th century, single-gender schools were common, but more importantly, education for women was limited to basic skills courses and did not include academic subjects that would lead to higher education. Therefore, early feminists urged access for all students to the entire academic curriculum, particularly the precollegiate academic subjects like math and science. Coeducational classes opened the doors to precollegiate study by girls and caused substantial increases in the enrollment of girls in colleges across the nation.

However, 50 years later, in the latter half of the 20th century, second-wave feminists decried inequities in male-dominated coeducational environments, particularly in athletics. It became apparent that within coeducational settings, secondary schools had organized single-gender physical education classes that routinely involved a lack of resources for female classes and teams. These secondary schools' arrangements mirrored and foreshadowed the inequitable allotment of funding for athletic teams at the collegiate level. In the early 1970s litigation surrounding these inequities coincided with other civil rights legislation. Ultimately, the federal government responded to the criticisms by attempting to provide equity through the provisions of Title IX (Tyack & Hansot, 2002), which specifically forbade separate class arrangements according to gender in physical education classes. School districts construed this prohibition to extend to academic classes. However, Salomone (2003) pointed out that the various statutory exemptions to Title IX "suggest that Congress did not intend to impose a sweeping ban on all single-sex education" (p. 184).

Over the last two decades, education policy makers have targeted declines in achievement among students of both genders. Sadker and Sadker (1995) claimed that schools were shortchanging girls, gaining the support of the American Association of University Women, which endorsed single-gender arrangements as a means of promoting female achievement, particularly in mathematics and science. However, within a few years, the American Association of University Women (1998) concluded that single-gender classes were potentially harmful for girls. Meanwhile, Sommers (2002) stated that single-gender arrangements were advantageous for boys who were found to be lagging in academic areas, particularly reading and writing. In general, however, advocates on both sides of the gender argument agree that the middle school years are the most critical time for the formation of habits that promote academic achievement (see Clewell, 2002).

In 2002, following the implementation of No Child Left Behind, the Office of Civil Rights began reviewing arguments about the legality of single-gender classes. This opened the door for schools to experiment with single-gender classes as a means of improving educational outcomes for their students. Such arrangements began to flourish throughout the nation, and within 18 months the Office of Civil Rights confirmed the legality of single-gender program options. Schools that had experimented with single-gender class arrangements found that after the initial flurry of controversy, the arrangements became rather routine among their student population. However, the question of the value and effectiveness of these arrangements remains open to research and discussion.

ASKING THE IMPORTANT QUESTIONS: SURVEYING THE ADULTS

Any reform must be examined from multiple points of view in order to capture "the essence of the experience" (Creswell, 1998) for all the stakeholders. The proverbial "elephant in the room" must be viewed through the multiple perspectives that result from the interaction of all the players with the elephant or, in this case, the reform that separated students into classes by their gender. Therefore, the complete study of this district's reform involved both qualitative and quantitative analyses, including classroom observations in both single-gender and mixed-gender classes and interviews with teachers (N = 12), students (N = 24), and parents (N = 7). Based on those interviews, surveys were administered to both students and faculty. In addition, quantitative analyses were conducted of the students' scores on Terra Nova achievement tests in 2002, 2003, and 2004. (Those findings will be discussed in detail in chapter 6.)

Classroom observations were conducted in both single-gender and mixed-gender classrooms. The observer noted some significant differences in the classroom environments. Students appeared to be more lively, more focused, and more on-task in the single-gender classes. Moreover, the teachers supported this observation and were generally favorably disposed to the single-gender arrangement. They reported differences in the responses of each gender to their work in those classes and observed that the single-gender arrangement allowed them to teach the students more effectively. Only one teacher, citing the need to promote diversity among the students, objected to the arrangement on a philosophical basis. Another speculated about the long-term effectiveness of single-gender classes, even though she could see the immediate positive results of the arrangement. Overall, however, most teachers interviewed were comfortable with the single-gender arrangement. Several reported that 6th-grade students of both genders appeared to be more relaxed in the single-gender arrangement, retaining behaviors that they had exhibited in 5th grade—for example, bringing stuffed animals or action toys to class. These behaviors were not observed in the mixed-gender 6th-grade classes.

A survey, constructed from responses to interviews with selected middle school teachers, was then administered to all the teachers in grades 6, 7, and 8. Table 1 summarizes key issues highlighted by the teachers.

Most teachers who responded to the survey (79 percent) felt that both genders seemed comfortable with the single-gender arrangement and that the single-gender arrangement allowed them to address the specific needs of each gender. Approximately half (54%) of the teachers expressed the need for in-service training to teach single-gender classes, but most (64%) felt that single-gender classes should continue to be an option for students

Table 1.   Teacher Survey (N = 28)

Survey Statement	Agree	Neutral	Disagree
Students are more focused and on-task in single-gender classes.	41%	40%	21%
Both genders seem comfortable with single-gender classes.	79%	14%	7%
In mixed-gender classes, students seek out same-gender friends for group projects.	79%	10%	10%
Girls and boys process information differently.	82%	11%	7%
Girls respond more in single-gender classes.	68%	21%	11%
Boys dominate in the mixed classes.	34%	14%	52%
Single-gender classes allow the teacher to address the specific needs of each gender.	68%	18%	14%
Teachers need in-service training to teach single-gender classes.	54%	17%	29%
I change my style to accommodate the gender I am teaching.	56%	7%	37%
Single-gender classes should continue to be an option for students and parents.	64%	18%	18%
I would choose to teach single-gender classes again.	61%	18%	21%

and parents and said that they themselves (61%) would teach single-gender classes again.

Parents who were interviewed and who had selected the single-gender option for their children were overwhelmingly pleased with the arrangement. They expressed satisfaction with their children's behavior and academic achievement. Most considered the arrangement to be beneficial both academically and socially for their children. However, one parent did express that it seemed to be working in the beginning of the school year for her child but that she had some concerns as the child had matured and become more social. Another parent, who had opted not to put her child in a single-gender arrangement, objected to the program on philosophical grounds. All parents interviewed emphasized their right to choose single-gender arrangements. Significantly, an overwhelming majority of all parents selected the single-gender option for their children in the following school year.

THE STUDENTS SPEAK:
INDIVIDUAL RESPONSES TO KEY QUESTIONS

It was the students' perceptions that provide the freshest and perhaps most honest appraisal of whether and how these arrangements might work for young adolescents. Middle school years typically involve tremendous development physically, emotionally, and cognitively. Therefore, it is not surprising that the students' interview responses varied according to their age. In general, the younger the student, the more likely that student felt positively about the single-gender arrangement. An in-depth view of selected student interviews across the three grades reveals the range of responses of the students according to their age and gender.

James, a slightly built 11-year-old boy in 6th grade, responded energetically to questions about his reaction to being in all-boys classes. His bright blue eyes twinkled as he admitted that his favorite class was gym class, "because you get to play games using your skills," but he noted that he didn't pay much attention to the girls in the universally mixed gym classes because he and his friends (all boys) liked to be on teams together.

James was equally candid about his involvement in his academic classes, noting that he felt "more challenged" in his all-boys classes. He explained that he enjoyed the competition with the boys in his classes: "I want to try to beat them. I didn't try to beat the girls [when he was in mixed classes] because I didn't think I could beat the top girls, so why bother?" His conclusion reinforces both research-based and empirical evidence of the developmental disadvantage experienced by boys in the middle grades.

Alison, also age 11 and in the 6th grade, said she "loves all-girls classes," especially math classes, because she's "good at math and won a stuffed animal in a math contest." Slight of build with deep brown eyes, she emphasized that she was happy she chose all-girls classes because "you don't have to worry about boys thinking on you or making fun of you." She reported that she participates more in all-girls classes, even though the level of the work seemed the same as what she did the previous year in her mixed 5th-grade class.

Becky, another 6th-grade girl, age 12, echoed Alison's concerns about emotional and intellectual safety in mixed-gender classes. She emphasized the freedom she felt in her all-girls class. She reported that she had asked her mother to enroll her in the all-girls classes because "the boys picked on me because I am smarter than them." She asserted that in all-girls classes the teachers "word things better and say them differently. In mixed classes they say things more simply for the boys." She felt that girls have the same ideas and can work well together, because the boys think of "disgusting things," especially in science. She added that all-girls classes are more fun and get more accomplished, even though the girls "get loud and ask too many questions." Her conclusion reinforces now-accepted conventional wisdom about the freedom experienced by girls in single-gender academic classes, particularly math and science.

Interviews with 7th-grade students revealed an anticipated shift toward adolescent emotional and social concerns, but those students also consistently remarked about their ability to focus more in their single-gender classes. Mary, age 13 and in 7th grade, reported that her mother suggested she try all-girls classes. She described herself as shy and quiet, but that she loves new things like a new language (Spanish) and new ideas in English, where she enjoys "expressing my feelings in poems." She thought she would just try all-girls classes for a year but had decided to stay with the arrangement because "I can concentrate better." She reported that she has seen a definite improvement in her grades because "I am not afraid to raise my hand. The boys picked on you and laughed at you if you got an answer wrong."

Nancy, age 12 and also in 7th grade, reinforced the emotional safety of single-gender classes. She reported that she thought all-girls classes would be "cool" because "you wouldn't be nervous to ask a question and be wrong—and then the boys might laugh at you." She also reported a significant increase in her grades: "We get higher grades because we pay attention more and don't get distracted." She planned to stay in all-girls classes in 8th grade because she couldn't think of any reason to change.

On the other hand, her classmate Heather, age 13, complained that she was in an all-girls class because "[m]y mom decided to torture me." She had no input into the decision but went along with it because she was curious. She conceded that she liked the all-girls classes because they made it easier to relate to her girlfriends, but added that all-girls classes allowed them to "help each other with guy problems." This observation clearly indicated her growing interest and relative preoccupation with adolescent social pairing. She further captured the essence of another aspect of the 7th-grade all-girls social environment when she said, "In some ways it's really nice to be with your friends, but sometimes the girls get really catty, and it is hard to get space away from them."

The boys in 7th- and 8th-grade classes were less enthusiastic about single-gender classes. Unlike their younger peers, they professed indifference to the arrangement at first, and then became more emphatically negative as the interviews progressed. Danny, age 13 and in the 7th grade, noted that he had been curious about all-boys classes, but now that he was in them, he planned to choose mixed-gender classes for 8th grade. He conceded that in the all-boys classes he could talk more about sports with his friends and "just hang out," but that in the single-gender environment, "[b]oys try to act tougher." Jim, also age 13 but in the 8th grade, felt that the school had organized all-boys classes "because of fights and stuff." He admitted that he had been picked on by other boys when he was in 7th grade, but that it was worse in the all-boys classes. He explained, "The guys who pick on us would be more interested in impressing the girls" in mixed-gender classes. He added that he missed his friends who are girls, because he can't rely on their friendship in the all-boys classes. His classmate Sam, also age 13, agreed that there was bullying in mixed-gender classes, but that there seemed to be more of it in the all-boys environment.

He personally enjoyed the all-boys classes because "I can concentrate more. The girls make too much noise." However, he suggested that the choice for single-gender classes should be for individual subjects and not all the academic classes, as had been organized by the school.

POLLING THE POPULATION: STUDENT SURVEY RESPONSES

The student interviews became the basis for a survey administered to all students in single-gender classes in grades 6, 7, and 8. Table 2 contains the array of all the responses to selected questions from the student survey, which was administered to students in all single-gender classes at the end of the first year of the arrangement.

Fifty percent of all students felt that they could concentrate more in single-gender classes, with the girls giving the most positive responses. In grade 6, 84% of the girls felt they could concentrate better in the single-gender classes, compared to 60% of the total 6th-grade population. However, 49% of all 7th-grade students said they could concentrate better in single-gender classes. Fifty percent of all 8th-grade students felt they could concentrate better in single-gender classes, compared to 70% of the girls in 8th grade.

Fifty-three percent of 6th-grade students reported that their grades had improved in the single-gender classes. Forty-six percent of all students

Table 2. Student Survey: Responses to Selected Survey Items by Girls and Boys in Grades 6, 7, and 8 Combined (N = 263)

Survey Statement	Agree	Neutral	Disagree
You can concentrate more in single-gender classes.	51%	21%	30%
You don't have to be afraid of being wrong in a single-gender class.	42%	35%	23%
Single-gender classes are quieter than mixed classes.	33%	14%	53%
You can act more like yourself in single-gender classes.	45%	27%	28%
Single-gender classes are fun because you can see your friends.	46%	27%	27%
Students should have a choice between single- and mixed-gender classes.	86%	11%	3%

felt that single-gender classes were fun because they could see their friends. This percentage declined by grade as the students grew into adolescence and interest in mixed-gender friendships: 57% of 6th-graders felt the classes were fun, as compared to 48% in the 7th grade, and 38% in the 8th grade.

Closer scrutiny of the survey responses revealed that positive reactions to single-gender classes were greatest in the 6th grade, dipped in the 7th grade, and increased dramatically in the 8th grade. Table 3 shows the differences in student responses according to their gender and grade.

Sixth-grade students were more positive on all key questions than their older peers, with the girls sounding a positive note across the board on all points. An astounding 84% of the 6th-grade girls stated they could concentrate more in all-girls classes, compared to 60% of the boys in those all-boys classes. Concentration in class was less important to both boys and girls in the 7th-grade, with less than half of those students overall (46%; 49% of the girls and 43% of the boys). However, while only 50% of all 8th-grade students felt they could concentrate more in their single-gender classes, 70% of the girls felt that the statement was true. Apparently the ability to concentrate among young adolescent girls regained importance among the oldest girls in the study. A similar pattern emerged from the students' survey responses when they were polled about their grades. When asked whether their grades had improved, 6th-grade girls

Table 3. Comparison of Responses by Grade and Gender

	Grade 6			Grade 7			Grade 8		
Survey Statement	*All*	*Boys*	*Girls*	*All*	*Boys*	*Girls*	*All*	*Boys*	*Girls*
I wanted to experience single-gender classes.	40%	29%	51%	24%	9%	35%	21%	8%	30%
You can concentrate more in single-gender classes.	60%	36%	84%	46%	43%	49%	50%	22%	70%
My grades have improved in single-gender classes.	53%	45%	67%	31%	23%	37%	33%	22%	41%
Single-gender classes are fun because you get to see your friends.	57%	52%	54%	48%	51%	46%	38%	46%	32%
I would choose single-gender classes again.	40%	21%	58%	30%	23%	35%	19%	10%	25%

agreed the most (67%), followed by the 6th-grade boys (45%) and then by 8th-grade girls (41%).

Boys, on the other hand, provided the most negative responses on the survey. When asked whether they had wanted to experience single-gender classes, only 9% of the 7th-grade boys agreed, followed by a low of 8% among the 8th-grade boys. In terms of the ability to concentrate, only 22% percent of the 8th-grade boys agreed compared to 43% of boys in the 7th grade and 36% of 6th-grade boys. Similarly low percentages characterize other key responses among the boys, especially when they were asked whether they would choose single-gender classes again. This item reached its lowest point among all 8th-grade students, but the condemnation of the 8th-grade boys was resounding. Overall, 19% of all 8th-grade students said they would choose single-gender classes again, but only 10% of the boys agreed to the statement. Among the girls, 25% of the 8th-grade girls would choose single-gender classes again, compared to 58% of the 6th-grade girls.

WHAT ARE THE STUDENTS TELLING US?

Age, gender, and social development have emerged as important consid-erations in the organization of single-gender classes in public middle schools. According to the students interviewed and surveyed, the majority in all grades stated that they could focus more in single-gender classes. However, students in the 6th grade were more open than the older students to the new single-gender arrangement at the start of the school year and more positive about it when the school year ended. Seventh-grade stu-dents felt the most negatively about the arrangement, verbalizing the im-portance of social concerns. On the other hand, 8th-grade students were more positive about the arrangement than the 7th-graders.

Not surprisingly, all students overwhelmingly felt that they should have the power to decide whether they would be in single-gender classes. The right to choose the organizational format of their classes was perceived as beneficial by both students and their parents. In fact, in the second year of the study, despite their responses on the survey, the majority of students opted to remain in their single-gender class arrangements. There were very few requests reported to switch to the mixed-gender classes, and these were offset by an equal number of requests from students in the mixed-gender classes to be assigned to the single-gender classes.

Single-gender class arrangements seem to have merit for students who are positively disposed to being involved in them, as long as they are given the choice to participate and the opportunity to opt out. The dynamics of that choice are open to further discussion and examination, however, since the return rate of the students seems to contradict the students' intentions on the survey. Since most students disagreed with the statement that they would choose single-gender classes again, it is likely that the parents made the final decision about choosing the single-gender classes for a second year. It is also likely that as the single-gender arrangement becomes more commonplace over time, the students will have a less negative response to the option.

It was apparent, however, that the younger the student, the more likely that student responded favorably to single-gender classes. Both in the interviews and the surveys that followed, students in the 6th grade reported more positive responses than students in the 8th grade. The language of the 6th-grade students revealed a preadolescent viewpoint of the inappropriateness of the behavior of peers of the opposite gender. Interestingly, 6th-grade boys and girls both referred to their opposite gender peers as "noisy" and "annoying."

Students of all grades reinforced the importance of emotional, intellectual, and physical safety, perennial concerns in the middle grades. The problem of bullying reared its head among the 7th- and 8th-grade boys, but the students who were interviewed did not agree on which arrangement might be less bully prone. Therefore, that problem seems to be endemic among the age, and, in this study, did not seem to be exaggerated by the single-gender classes in the first year of the study. However, caution dictates that further analysis might reveal a pattern of bullying emerging over time, especially in the all-male environment. The school must take measures to assure that a *Lord of the Flies* scenario does not emerge from a policy that keeps students in the same single-gender classes over the three years of middle school. Sorting students into different all-male configurations might address this problem, while keeping the single-gender arrangement.

On the other hand, the overwhelmingly positive responses among the girls in this study seem to indicate that single-gender classes are particularly beneficial to girls in the middle school grades. Once more, the younger girls were more positively disposed to the arrangement, but even the 8th-grade girls supported the notion of greater concentration in all-girls classes. The source of distraction by the opposite gender seemed to change over the grades. The younger students reported the noisiness of their opposite gender peers, both boys and girls. The older students simply referred to the social distractions of having opposite-gender peers in their classrooms. Not surprisingly, the older students loudly and clearly stated their preference for those distractions. As the girls became more socially aware and more adolescent, they also became more assertive about their interest in the boys. Unlike the boys, however, they expressed a feeling of bonding with their female classmates, to handle their boy issues together.

TAKING THE LONG VIEW

In 2003 the Office of Civil Rights opened the door to public discussion of single-sex classes in public schools according to the redefined parameters of Title IX. In 2006 the U.S. Department of Education confirmed the legality of single-sex classes and schools. The essential components of those parameters are the elements of choice and flexibility. Parents and students must be afforded a choice between single-gender and mixed-gender classes, and that choice must be offered equitably to both genders. There must be no distinction between the types of courses afforded to either gender. However, single-gender scheduling should be flexible within the school environment, allowing for variations in the organization of teams. This district displayed innovative programming by restricting single-gender classes to only the academic core courses. Offering subject-specific single-gender classes in each grade would provide even more flexibility within the existing school walls. Admittedly, this would stretch the limits of the traditional teaming concept, but when two equally good goals are at issue, creative and collaborative school administrators can and should design innovative educational environments that are not prescriptive but that meet the needs of the particular student population.

Turning Points (Jackson & Davis, 2000), a landmark document on middle school reform, recommended that schools offer multiple options to students in middle schools and involve the parents in the school experiences of their children. This is crucial in gaining the support of parents for any school initiative. The majority of parents in this district selected single-gender classes for their children. Conversely, however, the opportunity to choose also enfranchised the parents who chose mixed-gender classes. Having the ability to design by selection your child's education environment is an option not typically offered to parents in a public middle school.

However, the students in this study also reinforced the notion that they want to have input into the decisions that govern them. The older the students, the more definite was their insistence that they be consulted about the arrangement of their classes. Therefore, the timing of single-gender classes in middle schools emerged as the most important finding in this study. The youngest students seemed to respond more positively to the arrangement. Students in the 6th grade reported that they were more comfortable, more focused, and more successful academically in the single-gender classes. They seemed to enjoy their classes more and be less concerned about what might be happening in the mixed-gender classes. In fact, they seemed to act younger and react in more age-appropriate ways to their school environment without the social stresses of a mixed-gender class. This leads to the question of whether single-gender classes would be most effective in the 5th and 6th grades, while students complete their "intermediate" school years and before they enter full-blown adolescence.

By providing the option of single-gender environments within the existing school framework for students in the early middle years (grades 5 and 6), middle schools can also provide cost-effective school choice for parents, thereby involving them as stakeholders in the education of their children. Much of the rhetoric surrounding the school choice debate centers on the monolithic structure of the typical public school. Other issues, particularly those that involve staffing and facilities, often create obstacles for choice in a typical public middle school, especially in suburban and rural school districts where there is only one school to serve all students within the area. Creating single-gender classes for academic areas allows students to experience the benefits of single-gender classes, to interact with students of the opposite gender throughout the day, and to remain within the confines of one school building. It seems like a win-win situation for those who would choose this option. The only caution is echoed in the words of James, who warned us that he would "probably want to be with girls in high school." For some students, at some point in their early adolescence, single-gender classes provide a situation in which time flies, because students are having fun while learning with their same-gender peers.

REFERENCES

American Association of University Women. (1998). *Separated by sex: A critical look at single-sex education for girls.* Washington, DC: AAUW.

Clewell, B. (2002). Breaking the barriers: The critical middle school years. In E. Rassen, L. Iura, & P. Berkman (Eds.), *Gender in education* (pp. 301–313). San Francisco: Jossey-Bass.

Creswell, J. W. (1998). Qualitative inquiry and research design: Choosing among five traditions. Thousand Oaks, CA: Sage.

Jackson, A., & Davis, G. (2000). *Turning points 2000: Educating adolescents in the 21st century.* New York: Teachers College Press.

Sadker, M., & Sadker, D. (1995). *Failing at fairness: How our schools cheat girls.* New York: Simon & Schuster.

Salomone, R. (2003). *Same, different, equal: Rethinking single-sex schooling.* New Haven, CT: Yale University Press.

Sommers, C. (2002). Why Johnny can't, like, read and write. In E. Rassen, L. Iura, & P. Berkman (Eds.), *Gender in education* (pp. 700–721). San Francisco: Jossey-Bass.

Tyack, D., & Hansot, E. (2002). Feminists discover the hidden injuries of coeducation. In E. Rassen, L. Iura, & P. Berkman (Eds.), *Gender in education* (pp. 12–50). San Francisco: Jossey-Bass.

5

Going the Distance
Strategies for Teacher Preparation

Margaret Ferrara

SETTING THE STAGE

Today, the question *Why not separate-gender classrooms?* is being raised more frequently across the United States. Since the No Child Left Behind legislation opened the window of opportunity for single-gender classes, public school officials are asking this question more frequently. This interest has ignited sparks of reform in middle school education. Carol Gilligan (1993) spurred an initial interest with her research on feminist issues. She maintained, "Women . . . are oriented toward attachment, connectedness, and caring; [moreover] men . . . are oriented toward 'separateness' and abstract thinking" (in Salomone, 2003, p. 71).

Single-gender schools were once commonplace in the United States. Title IX legislation closed the doors of many of these schools. Today, single-gender schools currently exist as religious schools or elite independent schools. In public schools (peppered throughout the country), however, they are more the exception than the rule, possibly because the perilous condition of single-gender education in the United States is symptomatic of our national obsession with homogenizing education (Ruhlman, 1996).

The effectiveness of middle-level education is a hot topic. What to do? How to do it? No one disputes that middle-level learning is a critical time when students are in transition. Middle-level educators know that their students have needs distinctly different from elementary or high school students (Ecker, 2002). It is a time when students are changing physically, emotionally, and intellectually faster than at any other time in their lives. Ecker concludes that teachers must foster caring relationships between themselves and their students. It is also a time when students need to experience success and increase their self-esteem. Yet this growth needs to be structured with opportunities for choice and designed with an accountability plan. In this way, a school district's curriculum team can study what is working and what needs to be changed in order to foster effective learning.

"Middle-level students seem to be discouraged learners. Their whole beings are in turmoil, seeking to find that proper balance between their minds and bodies" (Tomlinson, Moon, & Callahan, 1998). As educators try to teach these students while they are in this turmoil, there is the added frustration of how to meet state and federal learning standards. This time is also compounded by the reality that middle-level students face comprehensive standardized tests in English language arts (ELA), science, social studies, and mathematics. In New York State, performance data for 8th-graders from 1999 to 2002 showed that students—at least those taking the state assessments—showed limited improvement in acquisition of knowledge standards prescribed by the Board of Regents. In the local school district, more than 50% of middle school students scored below an acceptable score in each of the four academic areas: English, mathematics, science, and social studies.

EXPLORING THE INITIATIVE

The school district tried many academic interventions, one of which was the implementation of single-gender classrooms as a 3-year experiment. The school district allowed parents to have the choice to place their children in single- or mixed-gender classrooms.

The idea of limited single-gender classes seemed to make "good sense." As one board member stated, "The idea does not cost extra money and we have a willing staff and community."

Data collected during the first year were largely focused on student performance, and indeed it was positive. Students in single-gender classrooms had improved attendance as compared to their attendance the previous year. In addition, the behavior referrals in single-gender classrooms decreased, most notably in the male classrooms. However, achievement data did not show a significant increase in achievement when 8th-grade student state assessment scores in ELA and mathematics were compared to 4th-grade scores from 4 years previous. However, report card grades did show a modest improvement.

Data were also compared by single-gender achievement as compared to mixed-gender classrooms. Initially, single-gender classrooms were similar in comparison, suggesting that students' learning arrangements do not necessarily make a profound difference in student academic achievement. The researchers then questioned, as did the school board and parents, What was possibly making a difference, especially in students' attendance and behavior? The tentative hypothesis proposed was teacher behavior.

WHAT ABOUT THE TEACHERS?

During the first year, teachers reported "stories" about how interesting it was to observe the differences in their all-male and all-female classes. Sometimes these stories were shared in staff development or department meetings. Teachers also shared their experiences when parents and administrators from other districts came to observe the single-gender classrooms. After the first year, teachers were asked about their insights through a formal survey. This was followed up by interviews and classroom observations. The emerging picture provided a clearer understanding of how single-gender learning influences learning and teaching and vice versa.

CAPTURING THE TEACHERS' VOICES

The qualitative study emerged from the need for teachers to share their insights. Questions were intended to be global so that teachers could express their insights and perceptions. In addition, the questions helped structure staff development for understanding gender differences based on research and effective teaching strategies. What were the perceptions of teachers on the success of the initiative? Would they want to be involved the following year? What worked in terms of strategies they discovered as they taught all-boys classes and all-girls classes? What would they like in terms of staff development if they wanted the single-gender learning arrangement to continue?

Surveys were distributed to teachers in June 2003 and more than 80% of the teachers (21 out of 28) involved in single-gender classrooms responded. Teachers who did not respond to the survey were special education teachers in resource rooms, and teachers in some of the specialized programs (e.g., music, home economics, computer lab). In these cases, the classrooms maintained a mixed-gender classroom format. The six-question survey form asked teachers to list the number of single-gender and mixed-gender classrooms they had taught in 2002–2003, the source of information given to them to learn about single-gender classrooms, and what they had learned about single-gender teaching and learning during the school year. In addition, the survey asked teachers what sources of knowledge they used during the school year, what information they would like to have to help them become more prepared to teach in single-gender classrooms the following year, and whether their opinion had changed about single-gender classrooms during the year. The survey questions were initially developed by two university professors and further refined by the building principal and the superintendent. In order to triangulate the data, interviews were conducted from randomly selected teachers in the three middle school academies, students from mixed- and single-gender classrooms, and the building principal. The interview questions centered on how teachers taught, how they assessed their students' learning, and what changes they had made in curriculum from the previous year when they had taught all mixed-gender classrooms. Students' interviews were focused on how they perceived what they found different in their instruction, learning arrangements, and assessment as compared to the previous year.

THEORETICAL FRAMEWORK

Despite a rich body of educational investigation that shows males and females act and learn differently in social settings (e.g., Lueptow, 1984, Sadker & Sadker, 1988), teachers often fail to appreciate the important difference gender makes in learning, especially when students are in a mixed-gender classroom (Sadker, 2002). Tomlinson (2001) found that because males and females learn differently, it is important to differentiate instruction. More males than females tend to prefer competitive learning, while females tend to prefer cooperative learning. The author, however, notes that it is important not to generalize these learning differences to all males or females. Differences in gender have also been associated with various tendencies in how students take in information, process information, and communicate their ideas. Researchers have also observed differences in how the two genders tend to express their information: Females tend to express themselves verbally, while males tend to express themselves through graphic representations (Schmuck, 1993).

Perceptions about gender differences have important implications for educational expectations by teachers, parents, and students themselves. Traditionally, males are expected to achieve well in mathematics and physical sciences, while females are more likely to be expected to achieve in English and social studies (Butler & Lee, 1998; Flood, Bates, & Potter, 2000). This trend, however, is changing and now girls are "catching up in math" (Conlin, 2003). Brain research has also supported findings that an average male is already developmentally 2 years behind females in reading and writing when he enters the first days of school. By grade 4, girls score higher nationally on reading tests than do males.

What brought the issue of gender differences to the forefront was the feminist movement of the last decade (e.g., Pratchler, 1996; Schmuck, 1993). Feminists argued that both female and male students need equal access to high-status knowledge such as science, mathematics, and technology. They also argued for the importance of presenting all students with a curriculum that offers models of excellence for males and females without any regard for their perceived abilities. This began an outgrowth, although limited, of single-gender classrooms (Blair & Sanford, 1999). The original purpose of single-gender classes was to provide opportunities for students, principally those in middle school, to focus more on their academic learning rather than on social concerns, and to provide "safe and comfortable" places where females may gain skills and confidence in the areas of mathematics, science, and technology. The outcome of this movement has been a closer look at what is taking place in the classroom and specifically in the academic learning of males and females.

FINDINGS

The survey and interviews yielded a high degree of information. Teachers reported that they received two research articles at the beginning of the school year about single-gender classrooms from the National Association for Single Sex Public Education (www.singlesexschools.org). One teacher reported, "We were just thrown into it with a little information and then it all just took off." During the school year, teachers found that they learned the most about effective strategies for single-gender classrooms from discussions with their colleagues and from insight gathered from parents or friends who had been in single-gender classrooms (e.g., in parochial school): "I read and discussed the topic with folks who knew it way back then, when it was not that unusual." A small percentage of teachers researched the education Web sites to gain more information, and some teachers shared their findings during faculty meetings.

One noteworthy finding from the survey is what teachers learned through their experiences in the classroom about what was effective for males versus females. It was typical for teachers to report that all-girls classes moved at a much faster rate and attained a higher overall class average than did all-boys classes. Girls found strength and leadership, another teacher reported, and the single-gender girls' classes were easier to teach. All-boys classes had mixed reviews. Few comments were made about the boys, but two female teachers found that in the single-gender boys' classroom, there was "too much adolescence in one room at one time" and that "boy classes tended to horseplay." To keep boys engaged, teachers found that they tended to call on boys more to respond to questions or to read a passage. On the positive side, teachers found that boys in single-gender classrooms reported they liked to do three quick activities rather than long, involved projects. One male reported that he wanted to go back to mixed-gender classes because he thought the girls were smarter and he would not have to give the teachers as many answers as he did in his all-boys classroom. Overall, teachers reported that boys and girls participated more and were less self-conscious about their work. Teachers also reported that boys' and girls' emotional reactions to success and failure are different. Boys enjoyed taking tests and girls enjoyed projects and writing stories. Both all-boys and all-girls classes enjoyed hands-on activities.

UP CLOSE AND PERSONAL

The delight of watching single-gender classrooms is that observations about differences are almost immediate. This has been evidenced during the second year of the study and was obvious to an observer who spent time watching the same lesson in both an all-boys class and an all-girls class. The lesson involved writing a structured book report on a biography that the students had read the previous week. The activity took place in the middle school library. All boys in the all-boys class wrote a report about a male figure: for example, a baseball or football player (for the most part). Girls, on the other hand, selected females as their topic in about 75% of the cases. These were typically female vocalists (e.g., Mariah Carey) or the tennis-playing Williams sisters. The males chosen were wrestlers or race car drivers. The girls talked about their choices with others at their tables and quickly completed their worksheets. The boys also completed their worksheets, but needed more prodding and coaching from the four adults in the room. In addition, the boys responded more to motivation techniques such as "I'll bet you a dollar you can't finish this by the bell," which some of the adults used to encourage them to complete their work.

Another way to look at differences is to compare learning tasks of students in a single-gender classroom to those in a mixed-gender classroom. The mixed-gender classroom was evenly balanced between the boys and girls. The lesson was on apple tasting and the objective of the lesson was for the student to rate the six apples in order from most favorite to least favorite. In the mixed-gender class, the differences were not apparent. In other words, students tasted the apples and quickly rated them. There was little discussion in the class among the students about the different apples. The activity took about 5 minutes total, and the students, for the most part, ate the entire apple section. Some girls did not eat the apple skin, but otherwise it was difficult to see how boys and girls differed in their responses. In the single-gender girls' classroom, the girls were much more tentative about making a judgment. They tended to nibble on each apple and rate with caution. They talked with the other girls in their area about their preference and gave reasons why they were choosing one apple over another. The activity took twice as long and the room was generally filled with a "hum" of discussion and reflection about their choices. In the end, the girls' rating sheets had been changed several times.

Sometimes the most direct way to learn about differences is to ask the students. Recently an Associated Press reporter visited the school; talked with teachers, administrators, and students; and wrote a press story about the single-gender classrooms at this school. The article spurred an interest in the state, and many small newspapers carried the story. One of the teachers brought the story from a small newspaper in the Adirondacks and read it to his all-girls class. He then asked them about their feelings about being in an all-girls class. The girls who responded were all pleased to be in this learning arrangement. Their comments indicated that they felt comfortable answering questions, they were not afraid to make a mistake when they answered a question, and they liked being able to work together and not having to compete with the boys. One girl admitted that it was also boring because there were no boys to talk to, or, as the teacher interpreted, "to flirt with."

Another observation worth mentioning is in watching teachers change their teaching strategies to meet the learning needs of boys and girls. A teacher found that she tends to teach faster, using "shorter bursts of information," to males to hold their attention. In contrast, she tends to allow girls to talk and even socialize to better develop their answers. Teachers also report that they tend to use less structure with girls and more with boys. Their awareness of gender differences influences how teachers structure their assignments. Teachers find that they repeat their deadlines for long-term assignments to the boys and provide more in-class time for them to work on long-term assignments. They tend to encourage girls to add creativity to their long-term assignments and do not spend as much class time on these assignments. Ironically, teachers find that their male classes are at least two to three classes behind their girls after a week on a thematic unit.

The statements that were the most interesting came from students. One student reported that she enjoyed being in an all-girls class because now she did not worry about her appearance as much. One day, she reported, she wore all orange clothes to school. She admitted that the different shades of orange did not match but it did not matter because she wanted to wear her favorite color. A teacher reported that at the end of the year, when she gave her all-girls class the consent form to return to the mixed-gender classroom for the next year, all the girls threw their permission slips in the wastebasket on the way out of the door.

Teachers found that even though they gained a wealth of information through teaching in single- and mixed-gender classrooms, they wanted additional information. The overwhelming request was for research studies on the topic, more information on curriculum and instruction, and gender-specific teaching strategies. Despite the limited information, teachers made adjustments in their teaching strategies by the end of the fall semester. They framed their classrooms to enable the girls to work more effectively in small cooperative groups, while the boys enjoyed a horseshoe desk arrangement where they could answer quickly and move on to hands-on activities. Girls tended to enjoy the project-based assignments, while boys tended to enjoy more competitive learning games and charts to show their progress. Teachers in mixed-gender classrooms also observed that students tended to pair off by gender if given the opportunity to select partners. The physical education teacher reported that on a few occasions when the boys and girls were separated for different activities, the boys and girls both participated more when they were in single-sex arrangements.

QUICK TIPS FOR GENDER DIFFERENTIATION

No set of teaching strategies for teaching males or females is foolproof. Admittedly, students learn differently based on more than their gender. Some researchers have found that differences in male and female learning styles are more subtle. For example, Feingold (1994) observed that girls tend to set higher standards in their classroom performance. Consequently, they self-evaluate their performance more critically. Ironically, with high standards, girls tend to have lower self-esteem, as they tend to be excessively critical in evaluating their own academic performance (Pomerantz, Alterman, & Saxon, 2002). Males, on the other hand, tend to have unrealistic estimates of their academic performance. The goal of the teacher is to help students look more critically at their learning goals and to self-evaluate themselves realistically. The points illustrated in table 1 are interesting characteristics that tend to be evidenced more clearly in single-gender classrooms and can be used as a baseline when setting up staff development programs.

The body of research on teaching strategies continues to evolve as teachers look at new ways of teaching (see www.singlesexschools.org/

Table 1. Single-Gender Learning Tips

Females	Males
Comfortable with cooperative learning arrangements; two females presenting to a small group is even more effective	Enjoy competition and challenges. As one writer explains, "Keep the classroom LOUD as compared with the girls' classroom and MOVING" (Taylor, 2002).
Enjoy assignments that are open-ended	Enjoy assignments that are "quick paced" and are completed quickly
Tend to report more verbally and engage more in classroom discussions	Tend to want to reach conclusions quickly and have more short-term discussions
Tend to add the arts (e.g., music, drama, and dance) to express feelings and concepts	Tend to use analogies based on sports or action figures to express concepts and less able to express feelings
Tend to express self more through fiction and poetry	Tend to express self more through nonfiction
Tend to enjoy role playing and skit development in order to summarize a concept or prior learning	Tend to enjoy activities that are objective and fact oriented in order to summarize a concept or prior learning (e.g., poster, model construction)
Tend to express activities that were done with parents and with friends	Tend to provide limited details about activities, and largely limited to activities with friends
Prefer assignments that involve reading	Prefer assignments that involve math or science
Prefer research and Web searches	Prefer computer challenging games (action games)
Prefer independent research projects	Prefer short reports
More comfortable with test formats that have short answers, extended prose, or verbal reasoning	More comfortable with test formats that have multiple choice and true and false
Tend to identify an academic failure as more than a failure of a subject; may generalize a failure of self and disappointment to others	Tend to identify an academic failure as a failure of a subject
Enjoy learning about the background of a concept or a skill before the concept or skill is taught	Tend not to be interested in the "story" behind the new concept or skill to be taught; tend to be more "just the facts" type of learner
Enjoy informal learning arrangements (e.g., first names, soft chairs, and pillows)	Work more effectively and with less discipline issues in classrooms that are formal (e.g., "Mr.")
Provide more text when asked to write a journal entry that begins, "I feel . . ."	Provide more text when asked to write a journal entry that begins, "I would like to be a . . ."
Tend to do better solving math word problems when they are embedded in a story	Tend to do better solving math word problems when they can be solved using spatial strategies

differences.html for recent research on this topic.) Teachers in single-gender classrooms provide wonderful insights into what is working and what needs to be changed. The newest challenge is to look at what has been learned in single-gender classrooms and take these lessons about differentiated instruction into mixed-gender classrooms.

IMPLICATIONS

Teachers consistently reported that it would take more than one year to observe the benefits and drawbacks of the single-gender classroom in depth. When asked if they would want to teach the following year in a single-gender classroom, 19 of the 21 teachers reported they would like to return to the single-gender classroom. One teacher remarked, "The differences are remarkable. Girls became more assertive socially. Boys are less affected by what is said in the classroom." Another teacher provided a unique insight when she wrote, "I realized that 6th-grade boys need a 'buffer' for their exuberance. I found out that in the mixed-gender classroom, it tends to be the 6th-grade girls."

The district professional development committee has been collaborating with a university partnership team to determine staff development workshops. Teachers will be asked to share what they learned the previous year. For example, for Shakespeare day the 6th-grade single-gender classrooms used *Julius Caesar* in the male classrooms and *Macbeth* in the female classrooms. When asked why the girls did not read *Romeo and Juliet*, the teacher responded, "We wanted a strong female character, and who other than Lady Macbeth?"

An area that is largely unexplored is specific instructional strategies or teaching models. One possible intention might be for the partnership team to observe students' learning in single- and mixed-gender classrooms to see the types of interactions, levels of questions, and learning materials. Based on the data, the team and teachers will explore alternatives. Teachers also will be provided with more material on brain-based research on males and females, differentiated instructional techniques, and specific articles on how boys as well as girls learn. It is imperative that practitioners engaged in teaching in single-gender as well as mixed-gender classes study their practice and continue to help students in all environments learn socially as well as academically.

REFERENCES

Blair, H., & Sanford, K. (1999). *Single-sex classrooms: A place for transformation of policy and practice.* ERIC ED433285.

Butler, D. A., & Lee, M. M. (1998). *Addressing gender differences in young adolescents.* ERIC ED441560.

Conlin, M. (2003, May 28). The new gender gap. *Business Week*, 75–82.

Ecker, M. (2002). Middle school still matters. *The School Administrator*, *3*(59), 30–33.

Feingold, A. (1994). Gender differences in personality: A meta-analysis. *Psychological Bulletin*, *116*, 429–456.

Flood, C., Bates, P, & Potter, J. (Eds.). (2000, November). Gender equity for males. *WEEA Digest.* ERIC ED450041.

Gilligan, C. (1993). *In a different voice: Psychological theory and women's development.* Cambridge, MA: Harvard University.

Lueptow, L. B.(1984). *Adolescent sex roles and social change.* New York: Columbia University.

Pomerantz, E., Alterman, E., & Saxon, J. (2002). Conceptions of ability as stable and self-evaluative process: A longitudinal examination. *Child Development*, *72*, 152–173.

Pratchler, J. (1996). *A voice for all students: Realizing gender equity in schools.* ERIC ED434891.

Ruhlman, M. (1996). *Boys themselves. A return to single-sex education.* (Quoting Diana Ravitch, p. 351). New York: Henry Holt.

Sadker, D. (2002). An educator's primer on the gender war. *Phi Delta Kappan*, *84*(3), 235–240.

Sadker, M., & Sadker, D. (1988). *Equity and excellence in education reform: An unfinished agenda.* ERIC ED302960.

Salomone, R.C. (2003). *Same, different, equal: Rethinking single-sex schooling.* New Haven, CT: Yale University Press.

Schmuck, P. (1993). *Gender equity: A 20-year perspective.* ERIC ED373423.

Taylor, D. (2002). Gender differences in informal education environments: A review of the literature on gender and learning in science museums. *Informal Learning, (52)*, 6–7.

Tomlinson, C. A. (2001). *How to differentiate instruction in mixed-ability classrooms.* Alexandria, VA: ASCD.

Tomlinson, C.A., Moon, T.R., & Callahan, C.M. (1998). How well are we addressing academic diversity in the middle school? *Middle School Journal, 29* (3), 3–11.

6

Does It All Add Up?

Single-Sex Classes and Student Achievement

Frances R. Spielhagen

INTRODUCTION

Do single-sex classes result in higher academic achievement? That is the question that drives research about the merits of single-sex education. Questions of social and emotional safety of students enter the dialogue, but the current educational environment mandates accountability and evidence-based practice. As a result, the potential of single-sex class arrangements to increase achievement dominates the discussion among educators striving to address declines in student performance, especially in the middle school years. At the same time, gut-level decision making often combines with political rhetoric to create a sense of urgency over the creation of such classes. Educators seek to structure the fragile learning environments of young adolescents, while parents focus on social situations that they feel can impede learning.

However, do single-sex classes produce the desired results—that is, higher standardized test scores? Simply put, the answer is a resounding "Yes," "No," and "Maybe." While single-sex classes are not a panacea for the social ills that beset young adolescents and impact their academic performance, recent research suggests that such arrangements work for some students, boys and girls, in some academic areas.

THE CONTEXT

Assessing the effectiveness of single-sex classes in middle schools is problematic because very often schools initiate many changes, including curriculum delivery and design, in an attempt to bolster declining achievement among students who are already in great personal and intellectual flux. Nevertheless, although it is difficult to attribute effectiveness and positive results to any one factor, specifically the segregation of students by their sex, single-sex arrangements can be examined and the results evaluated to get a greater sense of whether such arrangements are worthwhile. To explore the effectiveness of single-sex classes, I employed two statistical sources: standardized test scores and surveys of the teachers and parents of the students whose input I had already gathered (see chapter 3; see also Spielhagen, 2006).

How does one determine achievement? Certainly standardized tests comprise one acceptable measure. Therefore, I examined the standardized test results of 6th- and 7th-grade students in a small urban middle school (N = 600) in the Hudson Valley in New York State. Since a different test was used in 8th grade, I was not able to make any comparisons for students in that grade. Participation in single-sex classes in this middle school was voluntary. In the first year of the arrangement, parents were notified by mail that these classes were being created. Following the middle school "team" philosophy, all-girls and all-boys teams were established in each of grades 6, 7, and 8. Parents could opt out in writing on behalf of their children. More than 75% of the parents chose, by default, the single-sex teams. Interviews with students (see chapter 3) revealed that generally the students agreed with their parents' decisions on their behalf, and some had even participated in that decision making, so that most students in the single-sex classes had expressed a willingness to be included in these classes.

However, analyzing test scores is not enough in this environment, because they do not paint the complete picture of student performance. Consequently, I surveyed the teachers and the parents about their perceptions of the students' performance and achievement relative to the single-sex arrangements. The results of these surveys offer another means of understanding student behaviors and work habits, which contribute to overall achievement. In the fast-changing world of young adolescents, the perceptions of their parents offer a means of understanding the students' achievement in the midst of developmental change. The perceptions of the teachers provide an additional interface that reflects student performance in relationship to the increasing content demands of the middle school years. The teachers' experiences with middle school students over time inform their judgments about those students in the somewhat novel arrangement of the single-sex classroom.

LOOKING AT THE NUMBERS

Standardized testing is an annual event at this school. School officials used Terra Nova tests to predict student performance on the state's 8th-grade proficiency test and were eager to examine the efficacy of the single-sex classes. At their urging, I compared the annual Terra Nova scores of students in the first year of the single-sex program with those from the previous school year, when all students were in mixed-gender classes. I found gains in achievement throughout the data set, for students in both single-sex and mixed classes. Interestingly, these gains in achievement test scores were more pronounced in the 6th grade.

Overall, in the first year of the study, all students in grade 6 showed improvement on the Terra Nova tests over their performance in grade 5. Mean scores for students in grade 6 showed percentile gains (averaging 2 percentile points) in almost all academic areas. In two areas, percentiles stayed the same. The highest gains overall were in science and spelling. Each of these areas showed an increase of 6 percentile points, bringing both above the 50th percentile. Table 1 contains the analysis of test scores for all 6th-grade students. It is important to note that there were no declines overall in any content area and that improvements were noted regardless of whether the students were in mixed- or single-sex arrangements. Limitations within the data set prevented more detailed comparative analyses at the end of the first year of implementing the single-sex classes.

These results suggest two possible questions about other factors that might well be working together to produce the results that we found. First, did changes in curriculum delivery and/or awareness of curriculum delivery affect the ways in which teachers presented that information to the

Table 1.   Grade 6: Total Population (N = 114)

Content area tested	Grade 5: 2001–2002 Mean (SD)	Grade 6: 2002–2003 Mean (SD)	Change (+, –, =)	t	Sig.(2-tailed)
Reading	47.83 (28.7)	49.10 (28.3)	+	–.324	.747
Vocabulary	42.74 (28.9)	43.98 (25.8)	+	–.846	.399
Reading Comprehension	45.18 (29.7)	46.64 (28.1)	+	–.951	.344
Language	46.36 (28.9)	46.46 (28.6)	=	–.076	.939
Language Mechanics	39.06 (25.2)	42.16 (23.5)	+	–1.225	.223
Language Composite	42.21 (28.1)	44.43 (26.7)	+	–.968	.335
Mathematics	46.55 (26.5)	47.57 (28.1)	+	–.275	.783
Math Computation	45.30 (25.02)	47.57 (24.4)	+	–.829	.409
Math Concepts	45.92 (26.4)	48.10 (26.3)	+	–.786	.434
Total Battery	46.57 (27.6)	46.72 (29.3)	=	–.224	.823
Science	44.52 (28.8)	50.60 (25.2)	+	–1.524	.130
Social Studies	45.89 (27.7)	48.97 (27.4)	+	–.571	.569
Spelling	46.62 (29.1)	52.30 (28.9	+	–2.057	.042

students? Second, did the opportunity to select the type of class arrangement affect the way in which students approached their studies? In other words, because students had more control over how they were arranged, they might have interacted more readily and more eagerly with their course work.

Results were not as positive for 7th-grade students. Interviews with the 7th-grade students had revealed greater resistance to the single-sex arrangements. Therefore, not surprisingly, while grade 7 students showed improvement in specific areas of study over their performance in grade 6, 7th-graders did not exhibit the same global gains as their younger peers. Overall grade 7 percentile gains were in three academic areas (language, language mechanics, and mathematics) and remained virtually the same in three other areas (vocabulary, math computation, and math concepts.) Table 2 contains the overall analysis of all students in grade 7 who had been in the total population for both grades 6 (when all classes were mixed) and grade 7.

I returned to the school two years later, after the single-sex classes had been established for 3 years. When I examined the Terra Nova test scores of students during grades 5, 6, and 7, I found specific and perhaps more interesting results, with some limitations. Because the student population had changed over time due to normal attrition and change within the com-

Table 2. Grade 7: Total Population (N= 133)

Content area tested	Grade 5: 2001–2002 Mean (SD)	Grade 6: 2002–2003 Mean (SD)	Change (+, −, =)	t	Sig.(2-tailed)
Reading	57.77 (22.7)	56.62 (25.5)	−	.805	.422
Vocabulary	49.77 (23.8)	49.23 (24.5)	=	.302	.763
Reading Comprehension	54.02 (23.8)	52.77 (25.0)	−	.443	.658
Language	55.90 (26.8)	56.80 (26.2)	+	−.208	.836
Language Mechanics	55.90 (26.8)	44.36 (26.8)	−	1.067	.288
Language Composite	47.44 (25.96)	50.05 (26.9)	+	.702	.484
Mathematics	52.30 (26.95)	54.45 (27.6)	+	.540	.590
Math Computation	55.68 (27.7)	55.91 (26.8)	=	−.166	.868
Math Concepts	55.13 (27.5)	55.97 (27.6)	=	.283	.777
Total Battery	57.16 (25.1)	56.60 (26.7)	−	.346	.730
Science	57.07 (25.06)	54.33 (26.4)	−	.305	.761
Social Studies	55.64 (25.9)	54.13 (26.97)	−	.263	.793
Spelling	57.84 (25.5)	49.87 (26.2)	−	2.757	.007

munity, students not in school for all 3 grades were eliminated from the sample. This reduced the data set but made the comparisons possible.

However, a significant change in the data sample occurred because of one important factor that caused students to switch from single-sex to mixed arrangements in 7th grade: Students with higher test scores switched to mixed classes in order to take honors mathematics, offered only in mixed-gender classes to accommodate both boys and girls. The school had not created three separate honors-level math classes, one each for boys and girls and one mixed class. This was a clear example of how other organizational reforms within the school environment make it difficult to attribute changes solely to single-sex classes. Quite simply, the achievement scores in 7th grade were affected by the skimming off of the higher-ability students from the single-sex classes.

Despite these limitations, several interesting insights emerged about the performance of students in each of the arrangements. In reading, there were gains across the board for all students, regardless of whether they were in mixed- or single-sex classes. In math, scores declined in single-sex classes but increased for all students in mixed classes, with a notably large increase among girls in the mixed classes. This finding contradicts conventional wisdom about girls and mathematics classes. However, the fact that the 7th-grade mixed classes included the honors mathematics classes adds to our understanding of this change. The gains in mathematics quite logically derived from the sample of honors students in those mixed classes and the rigor of the curriculum. Students in the mixed mathematics classes started with higher scores and gained more over the year. Table 3 contains the percentile changes for all academic courses over the 3 years of the single-sex arrangement.

Students in the single-sex classes made the greatest gains on the language subtest. Students in mixed classes declined sharply (10 percentile points) in the language section of the test, with the sharpest decline among boys in mixed classes. There were gains on the total battery of the Terra Nova test, except among boys in the mixed classes and among all mixed students taken as a group, while girls in mixed classes virtually stayed the same from grade 5 to grade 7 on the total battery of the test, but made large gains in reading and mathematics. Table 3 contains the changes, both gains and declines, in percentile points on the Terra Nova tests over 3 years.

Several findings deserve further scrutiny, because at first they seem counterintuitive. In this school, analysis of the test results suggests that single-sex class arrangements clearly worked for some students. Test score gains reveal positive patterns of achievement in reading and language arts, especially as related to single-sex classes. However, gains in mathematics in the mixed classes may be related to curriculum and instruction in the honors-level class. Gains in language arts are most significant, but the decline in language scores in mixed-gender classes deserves further scrutiny. So, does it all add up? Additional analysis of other data provided further understanding of the effectiveness of single-sex classes through the lens of the adults who are stakeholders in organizing these classes.

Table 3. Percentile Changes on Terra Nova Tests in Year 3

	Reading	Math	Language Arts	Total Battery
Whole School	+1.7	−.85	+3.6	+1.4
Total Boys	+1.1	−1.2	+3.2	+.95
Total Girls	+2.3	−.49	+3.9	+1.8
All Students in Single-Sex Classes	+1.4	−1.6	+6.1	+2.0
All Students in Mixed Classes	+3.5	+5.6	−10.8	−1.5
Single-Sex Boys	+.80	−1.9	+6.0	+1.8
Single-Sex Girls	+2.0	−1.4	+6.3	+2.3
Mixed Boys	+2.9	+2.3	−11.1	−3.3
Mixed Girls	+4.1	+9.0	−10.4	+.28

THROUGH ANOTHER LENS

The students had already spoken clearly on surveys and in interviews of their opinions of the single-sex arrangements in their school (see chapter 3), but through their responses to surveys administered at the end of year 3, parents and teachers provided additional understanding about the perceived benefits of single-sex classes in this school.

The middle school teachers responded to a survey containing 30 statements regarding their experiences with single-sex classes and their opinions about the effectiveness of the arrangement for students. In general, the teachers felt both boys and girls were comfortable being with friends of the same sex and participated more in single-sex classes. Teachers noted positive effects for girls in single-gender classes and behavior problems and immaturity among the boys in single-sex classes. While the teachers acknowledged differences in learning styles between the girls and the boys, they also said they had changed their own teaching styles to accommodate each group.

The teachers were less positive about their role in teaching in the single-sex classes. They generally agreed that they needed in-service training to teach single-sex classes.

However, the teachers were split on whether the single-sex classes should continue: 44% agreed, 19% were neutral, and 37% disagreed that the school should keep the reform. Half of the teachers said they would teach single-sex classes again and one-fourth said they were neutral about the possibility. Another fourth said they would not want to teach single-sex classes again. Table 4 contains selected items from the teachers' survey with their responses.

Parents were also surveyed at the end of the third year. Not surprisingly, they expressed their concerns over the social pressures their children experience as young adolescents and their desire to stabilize the learning environment for their children. Most parents (63%) felt they were adequately informed about the single-sex arrangement. This is important since the informed consent of parents is critical in instituting this type of reform. A large number (49%) felt that single-sex classes help students learn better, but they were not decisive about whether single-sex classes provide a safer learning environment for children. An even larger number of parents (61%) felt that mixed-gender classes create more social

Table 4.   Teachers' Responses to Selected Survey Items at the End of Year 3

Statement	Agree	Neutral	Disagree
Girls are more social than boys in single-sex classes.	56%	33%	11%
Girls respond more in single-sex classes.	61%	22%	17%
Boys in single-sex classes act less maturely than they do in mixed-gender classes.	53%	5%	42%
Students are more focused and on-task in single-sex classes.	53%	5%	42%
Girls have shown sustained, positive growth in single-sex classes.	60%	33%	7%
Both genders seem comfortable with single-sex classes.	75%	13%	12%
There is greater participation by both genders in single-sex classes.	56%	6%	38%
Girls and boys process information differently.	69%	31%	0%
I focus on different aspects of the content with each single-sex class.	19%	25%	56%
I change my style to accommodate the gender I am teaching.	50%	25%	25%
Teachers need in-service training to teach single-sex classes.	44%	44%	12%
Single-sex classes should continue to be an option for students and parents.	44%	19%	37%
I would choose to teach single-sex classes again.	50%	25%	25%

pressure than single-sex classes, but many (51%) also felt that mixed-gender classes help children learn how to function in the real world. A large number of parents (59%) also felt that single-sex classes should continue to be an option at this middle school, and many (46%) would choose single-sex classes again for their children. Table 5 contains the survey items and parents' responses.

THE BOTTOM LINE

Does it all add up? Are single-sex classes effective? That depends on the criteria that determine effectiveness. If test scores are the benchmark, then the results of this study suggest that single-sex classes work for some students in some classes, but do not guarantee increased achievement performance on standardized tests. However, teaming considerations and hon-

Table 5. Parents' Responses to Survey Items at the End of Year 3

#	Statement	Agree	Neutral	Disagree
1.	I was adequately informed about the option of single-gender classes for my children.	63%	16%	20%
2.	I have had experience with single-sex classes myself as a student.	17%	18%	65%
3.	I wanted my child to be in single-sex classes.	51%	24%	25%
4.	My spouse/partner agreed with my decision about single-sex classes.	56%	32%	12%
5.	My child agreed with the decision we made about single-sex class placement.	60%	21%	19%
6.	Single-sex classes help students learn better.	49%	26%	25%
7.	Single-sex classes provide a safer environment for children.	38%	38%	24%
8.	I have seen an improvement in my child's school achievement because of single-gender classes.	29%	43%	28%
9.	My child has enjoyed single-sex classes.	36%	42%	22%
10.	Mixed-gender classes create more social pressure than single-sex classes.	61%	18%	21%
11.	There is more bullying in single-sex classes than in mixed classes.	31%	42%	27%
12.	Single-sex classes allowed my child to stay younger longer.	22%	56%	22%
13.	Mixed-gender classes help children learn how to function in the real world.	51%	30%	19%
14.	I would choose single-sex classes again.	46%	22%	32%
15.	Single-sex classes should continue to be an option at Ellenville Middle School.	59%	25%	16%

ors tracking clearly affected the test results in this school. These organizational concerns in middle school also muddied the waters and render clear conclusions difficult at best. Therefore, based on the test scores examined, no definitive statement can be made about the effectiveness of this school's single-sex classes in raising test scores across the entire population.

If single-sex classes do not guarantee increased achievement in the naturally volatile social environment of young adolescence, then other means of examining efficacy were considered. The opinions of teachers and parents provided another way of assessing whether single-sex classes are effective. Their responses also suggested that single-sex classes work for some students in some situations. Though not a panacea for all students in middle school, single-sex classes, according to adults who witnessed their implementation over 3 years, offer one way to create a safe and positive learning environment for some students.

CONCLUSION

Young adolescents are complex and varied in their development physically, cognitively, socially, and emotionally. Educators who grapple with meeting the needs of middle school students are considering multiple delivery models to address the complexity that defines the population. From 2002 to 2006, single-sex classes increased throughout the nation, reaching at least 241 in 2006 (Vu, 2006) according to Stateline, an organization that tracks educational changes across the nation.

In the middle school years, choice and ownership are critical to the development of young adolescents into autonomous learners. Jackson and Davis (2000) strongly recommend the involvement of the students and their parents in decision making involving school arrangements for the students. Students who opt for single-sex classes may benefit from the arrangement simply because they chose it. However, their success may well be related to the chicken/egg symbiosis of choice and efficacy.

Should all middle students be taught in single-sex classes? Of course not! The very complexity of the middle-school population precludes any "one size fits all" approach to education at this level. However, the more pertinent question is whether single-sex classes should be offered as a viable choice for students, parents, and teachers who strongly favor them and want to be involved in them. The answer to that is a resounding "Yes." In the complex world of the middle school, single-sex classes provide one way of addressing the developmental needs of some of the student population. In this school, single-sex classes seemed to benefit the students who were positively disposed to being involved in them. Moreover, the success of the single-sex classes was connected to the developmental stages of the students. The younger the students, the more positive their responses to the single-sex classes and the greater their gains on achievement tests. The bottom line is that in this school, single-sex classes provided opportunities for success among the students involved in them.

REFERENCES

Jackson, A., & Davis, G. (2000). *Turning points 2000: Educating adolescents in the 21st century.* New York: Teachers College Press.

Spielhagen, F. (2006). How 'tweens view single-sex classes: Students talk about some benefits—and some drawbacks—of single-sex classes. *Educational Leadership, 63*(7), 69–75.

Vu, P. (2006, September 19). Single-gender schools on the rise. Stateline.org. Retrieved September 21, 2006, from www.stateline.org.

7

Good News and Bad News
Student Behavior in Single-Sex Classes

Margaret Ferrara and Peter Ferrara

SINGLE GENDER—LOOKING BACK—LOOKING AHEAD

In the past 5 years, there has been an extraordinary surge of interest in single-gender public education. The most important factor driving this resurgence is the growing recognition that there are clear differences in learning in a single-sex environment and that these differences might affect positively the discipline of students in schools, especially in our public middle schools (NASSPE, 2006).

Historically in the United States, single-gender schools for the most part enjoyed status as a symbol of quality education usually not found in a coeducational environment. These coeducational public schools by default addressed the needs of indigent populations (Kaminer, 1998). Exclusivity, however, had its price: The cost of maintaining separate facilities became prohibitive, and by the end of the 19th century, only 12 of the 628 public school districts in Boston, for example, had single-gender schools (Shmurak, 1998). By the 1970s even affluent private schools, driven by prohibitive costs, began to follow the survival trend of becoming coeducational. By 1980, putting the financial excuse aside, single-gender education lost its luster and became a barrier against normal adolescent socialization (Lee & Bryk, 1986).

Despite the many years of single-gender education in this country in exclusive, private settings, there appears to be no meaningful consensus as to whether or not it is beneficial for students enrolled in public schools.

This ambivalence comes from the fundamental lack of applicable data. Eight years ago, only 4 public schools in the United States offered single-gender educational opportunities. As of April 2006, at least 209 public schools in the United States are offering gender-separate educational opportunities (Sax, 2006). Most of those are coeducational schools that offer single-gender classrooms in which students have the option of either single-sex or coeducational classrooms, retaining at least some coeducational activities (in some cases, only lunch and certain electives). Forty-four of those 209 schools are completely single gender in format and 165 offer single-gender classrooms (NASSPE, 2006).

Most single-gender programs in the United States are in private academies with stringent entrance requirements grounded in difficult entrance examinations coupled with high tuition costs. These schools, with their elite students, limit any meaningful comparisons and applicability of single-gender study findings to public schools. Additionally, Title IX, the federal law that prohibits sex discrimination in education institutions, generally discourages the formation of single-gender public schools. This leaves researchers with relatively little access to data that could better inform public policy decisions (Caplice, 1994).

The turn back toward single-gender education began in 2001, when Sen. Kay Bailey Hutchison along with Sen. Hillary Clinton, who originally proposed new legislation legitimizing single-gender education in U.S. public schools at a Democratic fund-raiser in 2001, successfully passed a bill to allow single-sex classrooms in schools. Their proposal became law.

> There should not be any obstacle to providing single-gender choice with the public school system. We should develop and implement quality single-gender educational opportunities as a part of providing diversity of public school choices to students and parents. Our long-term goal has to be to make single-sex education available as an option for all children, not just for children of parents wealthy enough to afford private schools. (Clinton, 2001)

The growing popularity of single-gender classes has also gained momentum in other countries, namely Australia, New Zealand, the United Kingdom, and Ireland. The question remains: Do single-gender classrooms really make a difference?

EXPLORING THE QUESTION FROM A FOCUSED PERSPECTIVE

Researchers have attempted to measure single-gender classroom success in many ways, namely through academic achievement, attendance, social learning, and self-esteem. Given the variety of goals and desired outcomes that can measure single-gender success, it is still difficult to answer the question *Does single-gender schooling work?* Before one can answer this question, the areas in which improvement are sought must be clearly defined.

Researchers have selected different indicators for success based on their hypotheses of what single-gender education can do for students. These indicators generally fall into two broad categories: attitudinal and academic. Attitudinal studies include studies in social identity (e.g., Murphy & Ivinson, 2000), self-esteem (e.g., Foon, 1988) gender student preferences (e.g., Gilbert & Gilbert, 1998), attitude toward subject areas (e.g., Rowe, 1988), and gender response to the classroom curriculum (e.g., Sadker & Sadker, 1994). Academic areas focus on achievement and a general environment that is conducive to scholastic achievement (e.g., Kleinfeld, 1999).

An argument against single sex-classrooms is that mixed-gender classrooms "support classroom social organizations" and that including girls in classrooms helps with boys' "rough behavior" (Sadker & Sadker, 1994, p. 18). In contrast, proponents of single-sex classrooms believe that separating boys and girls is instrumental in reducing male and female levels of distraction and peer pressures (Datnow, Hubbard, & Woody, 2001). This research also suggested that the single-sex classroom environment is just one of many factors that influence social organization in a classroom (Datnow, Hubbard, & Woody, 2001).

BUILDING FROM A RESEARCH PERSPECTIVE

Data reported in a school district in Seattle showed a significant decrease in students' discipline referrals in a single-gender environment. These data seem to suggest that single-gender schools do provide an environment conducive to acceptable student discipline. Davis (2002) reported that in the same school district, the principal of an elementary school found that discipline referrals to his office dropped from 30 a day to 2 or 3. In addition, the principal found that only 10% of male students met state-acceptable benchmark testing standards the year prior to the implementation of single-sex classes. With single-gender classes, that number rose to 73%. The principal did acknowledge, however, that there was no formal research in place to verify this phenomenon. He hoped to plan a more structured action research project for the 2002–2003 school year.

Research studies are not quite clear about the influence of a single-gender school arrangement on student discipline. A belief often proposed against single-sex schools is that "boys need male teachers and girls need female teachers" in order to have a good gender match between students and teachers. Researchers have not been able to demonstrate that this belief is the answer. Some found in a few cases that teachers' attention to gender-related issues made students feel uncomfortable even when the teachers were of the same sex as the students (Datnow, Hubbard, & Woody, 2001). This was in contrast to a research report in Belgium where girls in single-sex schools, as compared to girls in coeducational schools, perceived their schools as placing a stronger emphasis on order and control (Brutsaert & Van Houtte, 2004). Another finding was that in all-girl schools, there was a larger presence of female teachers and that these teachers tended to be more insistent on discipline and general order. Another interesting finding showed that males and females in single-gender schools perceived their schools to have more of an academic emphasis than did those in coeducational schools.

TRYING TO FIGURE IT OUT

In a rural school district in New York State, the superintendent of schools initiated single-sex classes in the middle school, grades 6 through 8. The Board of Education, the administration, and the school community, including the students, were enthusiastically in favor of this change from the traditional middle-school grade configuration.

The superintendent and his staff initiated a 3-year study to explore the effects of single-gender academic classrooms in grades 6, 7, and 8 of the middle school. Data collection began during the fall of 2002 and ended in the fall of 2005. The study explored the differences among students in coeducational classrooms compared to students in single-gender classrooms in terms of discipline and daily school attendance.

At the beginning of the study, there were 138 students in the 6th grade, consisting of 79 males and 59 females. The 7th grade had 78 males and 75 females, for a total of 153 students. In the 8th grade, 159 students were divided almost evenly—81 males and 78 females. These students, in concert with their parents' approval, chose required subjects taught in single-gender classes. The principal assigned students to classes in English, math, science, and social studies as evenly as possible, allowing sufficient classes for those students who chose not to participate in the single-gender study. Once the principal and the faculty completed the scheduling, there were five single-gender classes in the 6th grade, with an average class size of 23 students, and two dual-gender classes of 13 students each. In the 7th grade, there were six single-gender classes averaging 20 students in a class, with two coeducational classes of 13 and 14 students. Six single-gender classes made up the 8th-grade class of 159 students, along with two coeducational classes, one class with 6 students, and the other with 21 students. The principal attributed this disparity to scheduling issues.

One way to look at the data is to compare the data from the preimplementation phase with the data from the single-sex environment. Table 1 captures the profile of males the year before the change to single-sex classrooms.

The highest areas of infractions were class disruptions, being tardy to class, being uncooperative, and insubordination to teachers. In the traditional classroom, 8th-grade males had the highest number of these infractions, with 7th- and 6th-graders close behind. Table 2 shows the number of the same infractions for males in single-sex classrooms.

The data show that there was an overall 22% reduction in infractions (N = 289). The largest decrease in infractions was in the 6th grade, with 74% fewer reported infractions, followed by the 7th grade (37%) and the 8th grade (21%). The study did not corroborate the types of infractions most frequently identified by teachers and administrators: disrupting class (3%), insubordination (14%), and being uncooperative (14%). The study found that these infractions were not statistically significant. However, the study did find a more positive outcome in the decrease in infractions that appear to influence academic learning: tardiness (64%), incomplete assignments (63%), being unprepared (28%), and disrespecting peers (15%). There was a decrease in behaviors that typically result in school

Table 1. Male Behavior Problems in Mixed-Gender Classrooms

Totals	Infractions	Grade 6	Grade 7	Grade 8
1	Behavior	0	0	1
85	Bus Referral	13	35	37
20	Criminal Mischief	7	6	7
24	Cut Detention	3	1	20
29	Cutting Class	6	7	16
4	Danger to Self/Others	2	2	0
91	Disrespectful to Peers	30	38	23
21	Disrespects Others	8	6	7
321	Disrupting Class	100	121	100
32	Incomplete Assignment	1	23	8
122	Insubordination	27	44	51
84	Intimidation	26	23	35
3	Lunch Misbehavior	1	2	0
35	Other	11	7	17
25	Profanity	6	12	7
4	Sexual Offenses	2	0	2
178	Tardy to Class	2	62	114
2	Theft	0	1	1
5	Truant	0	1	4
122	Uncooperative	28	56	38
43	Unprepared	8	14	21
46	Verbal Abuse	22	16	8
1300		**304**	**479**	**517**

suspension: truancy (80%), cutting detention (71%), bus referrals (67%), and criminal mischief (40%).

In an analysis of grade-level infractions, 6th-grade male infractions decreased by 75%. This was the greatest decrease as compared to the data of 7th- (37%) and 8th-grade males (21%). Sixth-grade males showed the greatest decrease in behaviors that negatively affected classroom learning and usually resulted in school suspensions:disrespecting peers (100%), insubordination (93%), being uncooperative (89%), and disrupting class (84%). Sixth-grade males had a slight increase (by seven incidents) in detention for "cutting" classes, completing assignments, profanity, and tardiness. The data for 7th-grade males showed a most interesting decrease in the number of reported class disruptions (47%) and tardiness (50%). Eighth-grade males' level of infractions increased in two areas that affect academic learning: classroom disruptions (46%) and incomplete assignments (N = 8 to 42, a 425% increase). There was also a marked decrease

Table 2.   Male Behavior Problems in Single-Sex Classrooms

Totals	Infractions	Grade 6	Grade 7	Grade 8
2	Behavior	0	0	2
29	Bus Referral	0	14	2
12	Criminal Mischief	0	2	3
7	Cut Detention	7	3	1
41	Cutting Class	1	16	19
2	Danger to Self/Others	0	0	0
77	Disrespectful to Peers	0	21	26
10	Disrespects Others	1	2	0
310	Disrupting Class	16	64	146
12	Incomplete Assignment	3	7	4
105	Insubordination	2	36	42
79	Intimidation	27	25	28
8	Lunch Misbehavior	0	0	7
31	Other	1	12	8
21	Profanity	2	8	7
2	Sexual Offenses	0	0	0
65	Tardy to Class	9	31	32
3	Theft	0	1	2
1	Truant	0	1	0
105	Uncooperative	3	32	47
31	Unprepared	3	16	7
54	Verbal Abuse	0	9	23
1011		**75**	**300**	**407**

in the number of bus referrals (95%), cutting classes (95%), insubordination (47%), and tardiness to class (72%).

Data changes in the female profile shared comparable findings. Table 3 captures the profile of females in traditional classrooms the year before the study.

The most frequently cited infractions for girls were comparable to male infraction data: tardiness, insubordination, classroom disruptions, and being uncooperative in the classroom. Teachers in traditional classrooms reported more than 60% fewer infractions for girls as compared to males. Interestingly, the data showed that the areas with the highest number of infractions were the same as for males: tardiness, disrupting class, insubordination, and being uncooperative.

As illustrated in table 4, after the first year, collected data show that females had a 35% decrease in overall disciplinary infractions. Data for 6th-grade females showed a 95% decrease, and the 8th-grade female data showed a 28% decrease. Seventh-grade females had a 5% decrease in in-

Table 3.   Female Behavior Problems in Mixed-Gender Classrooms

Totals	Infractions	Grade 6	Grade 7	Grade 8
0	Behavior	0	0	0
29	Bus Referral	7	4	18
6	Criminal Mischief	1	3	2
11	Cut Detention	1	2	8
27	Cutting Class	9	7	11
0	Danger to Self/Others	0	0	0
22	Disrespectful to Peers	4	8	10
5	Disrespects Others	1	0	4
71	Disrupting Class	20	32	19
10	Incomplete Assignment	1	6	3
56	Insubordination	28	2	26
4	Intimidation	4	0	0
1	Lunch Misbehavior	0	0	1
40	Other	11	10	19
8	Profanity	3	4	1
0	Sexual Offenses	0	0	0
161	Tardy to Class	12	26	123
0	Theft	0	0	0
0	Truant	0	0	0
35	Uncooperative	8	11	16
16	Unprepared	1	6	9
15	Verbal Abuse	6	5	4
517		**117**	**126**	**274**

Table 4.   Female Behavior Problems in Single-Sex Classrooms

Totals	Infractions	Grade 6	Grade 7	Grade 8
0	Behavior Injury	0	0	0
9	Bus Referral	1	3	5
2	Criminal Mischief	0	2	0
4	Cut Detention	1	1	2
38	Cutting Class	0	10	28
0	Danger to Self/Others	0	0	0
7	Disrespectful to Peers	0	1	6
6	Disrespects Others	0	2	4
53	Disrupting Class	2	3	48
1	Incomplete Assignment	0	1	0
39	Insubordination	0	13	26
7	Intimidation	0	2	5
2	Lunch Misbehavior	0	2	0
23	Other	0	10	13
2	Profanity	0	1	1
1	Sexual Offenses	0	0	1
81	Tardy to Class	1	51	29
0	Theft	0	0	0
2	Truant	0	1	1
24	Uncooperative	0	5	19
15	Unprepared	1	7	7
6	Verbal Abuse	0	3	3
324		**6**	**120**	**198**

fractions. In a closer look, there were some interesting findings. In the area of tardiness, 6th- and 8th-graders had a 92% and 72% decrease in these infractions, respectively. In contrast, 7th-grade female data showed a 96% increase in tardiness. Sixth- and 7th-grade female data showed a decrease in insubordination infractions (100% and 48%, respectively). However, the 8th-grade female data of girls in the single-sex classrooms showed the same number of infractions as when they were in the traditional classrooms. In the classification of classroom disruptions, 6th- and 7th-grade females had a 90% decrease in the number of classroom disruptions; 8th-grade females had a 29% increase. This was also true in the area of being uncooperative, where 6th- and 7th-grade female students had a decrease in infractions and 8th-grade females had a 16% increase in infractions.

CONCLUSIONS: LOOKING
TOWARD FUTURE RESEARCH IN THIS AREA

These data, although not conclusive, provide a peek into what may be possible in a single-sex school environment, especially for middle school students. The data, at a minimum, hint that students in a single-sex environment may learn with fewer disciplinary issues than when they are in the traditional school configuration.

There were challenges in this study. The first challenge was to ensure a consistent data set. For example, teachers and administrators did not code infractions in the same manner from year to year because the state requirements often change. Another challenge dealt with a reluctance to make discipline infractions known to the school community and the public at large. This is not just a local problem, but one that is prevalent throughout our country's school districts. James Garbarino, a psychology professor at Loyola University in Chicago, said that "he and other school violence experts are skeptical about watch lists that are based on self-reporting, which essentially amounts to an honor system." He added, "[L]ots of schools don't want to report because it brings unwanted negative attention. It affects the careers of school administrators and school boards, and it can even affect real estate values. So there is a lot more at work here that just acts of violence" (Hu, 2006, p. 28).

Another challenge was to ensure a balance in the number of students in each group. In fact, the class size numbers in the control group (the mixed-gender classes) and in the single-sex classes proved to be highly disparate. Based on the low number of students in the control group, it was not possible to draw conclusive findings about the effect of single-sex classrooms on the number of student disciplinary classroom infractions.

A change in administration precipitated the fourth challenge, 2 years into the study: The school administration cancelled the study, thereby eliminating the continued collection of single-sex related data by the researchers. However, the data collected do provide some interesting points for discussion. One point is that males, no matter what the setting, tended to initiate more disciplinary infractions than females. In addition, females in 7th grade (in this school) tended to commit more infractions than females in 6th or 8th grades. Finally, males and females appeared to have high and comparable numbers of infraction types in three main areas: tardiness, insubordination, and classroom disruptions.

There are additional interesting answers to seek in subsequent single-sex research studies. Was there is a significant decrease in classroom infractions related to the change in classroom structure—from the traditional arrangement to single sex? Does teacher bias about gender result in different treatment of students, either boys or girls?

It is difficult to determine whether teachers interpret students' behavior in a gender-specific way and then make a decision to either report the infractions or allow them to go unreported. On the other hand, the data do demonstrate that infractions were somewhat reduced during the first year of the implementation of single-sex classrooms. Was this the Hawthorne Effect? Maybe! Future research may provide more substantive answers. There does appear to be some positive outcomes for learning in the middle grades in a single-sex environment.

In conclusion, the issue of single-sex classrooms demands more research. First, researchers need to be clear and exact in their explorations of interventions of academic achievement, discipline, or self-esteem. Secondly, they must draw their data from quantitative statistics as well as qualitative sources. Finally, they must explore other essential features that affect their findings, namely race/ethnicity, socioeconomic level, and teacher competency. The limitations of this study did not permit the researchers to examine these impacts as they related to a single-gender school environment.

Some studies reviewing the impact of single-sex classrooms indicate that there was a short timeline for actual preparations. This was true in this study. The short timeline for implementation was due to the inability of the decision makers to give the "go ahead" with the project. After all, the single-sex classroom structure is a departure from many years of the same configuration. A year for general planning is vital. Teacher training is vital to ensure an understanding of the special needs and abilities of each gender.

Parents tend to be attracted to the single-sex classroom environment, seeing it as an opportunity for their children to benefit from special ways of learning and to reduce distractions from the opposite sex. In this study, parents did not mention that they chose the single-sex learning arrangement because they saw it as an opportunity for gender equity for their children.

This study also found that teachers in the single-sex classroom reinforced traditional gender stereotypes. Teachers tended to provide instruction for boys in a more regimented, traditional, and individualist fashion and girls in a more accepting, cooperative, and open environment.

There is a paucity of research conducted in single-sex classrooms reagarding teachers and their perceptions about classroom management techniques. It would be interesting to have teachers study their own practice in single-sex classrooms on how they decide what is an infraction and when an infraction merits discipline.

The sustainability factor is important in the case of a single-sex classroom school. In some cases, there are other complexities, such as difficulty with scheduling single-sex and mixed-gender classrooms, teacher nonacceptance of single-sex classrooms, or a lack of community support over time. In any case, without sustainability, it is difficult to provide any conclusive evidence that single-sex classrooms provide a positive effect on classroom learning. Evidence, albeit inconclusive, continues to suggest that single-sex classrooms paired with other interventions can enhance the learning environment for all students.

Discipline of students in our schools is an urgent issue. Not a day goes by without some mention of student discipline issues in our media. Unfortunately, there have always been discipline issues in schools, usually reflective of the times. In 1915, for example, our world was not fast-paced as it is today. At that time few, if any, discipline records were kept as we have today. Just look at our No Child Left Behind school accountability reporting for each state; there are at least 22 categories of discipline infractions that must be kept by each school and reported in a consistent and uniform manner. The problem is that there are too many reporting inconsistencies, which can easily bias the data. Even 20 years ago, students respected educators more, parents supported the schools (what the teacher said was accepted as true), and the schools were accepted as safe havens. Students did not have the outside distractive forces of the Internet, cell phones, and our numerous micro toys.

The implementation of single-sex classrooms as an intervention may be one answer for meaningful learning within our classrooms. We must continue to review single-sex research as a potential answer to the perennial and pressing question of why so many of our students are not learning as well as they should while they are in school.

REFERENCES

Brutsaert, H., & Van Houtte, M. (2004). Gender context of schooling and levels of stress among early adolescent pupils. *Education & Urban Society*, *37*(1), 58–74.

Caplice, K. (1994). The case for public single-sex education. *Harvard Journal of Law and Public Policy*, *18*(1), 227–292.

Datnow, A, Hubbard, L, & Woody, E. (2001). Is single sex schooling viable in the public sector? Final Report. ERIC ED471051.

Davis, M. (2002, May 15). Department aims to promote single-sex classrooms. *Education Week*. http://www.singlesexschools.org/ew/articles/2002/05/15/36gender.h21.html. Retrieved June 5, 2006.

Foon, A. (1988). The relationship between school type and adolescent self-esteem, attribution styles, and affiliation needs: Implications for educational outcome. *British Journal of Education Psychology*, *58*, 44–54.

Gilbert, R., & Gilbert, P. (1998). *Masculinity goes to school*. London: Routledge.

Hu, W. (2006, October 8). A very violent school, or just very honest about reporting its violence? *New York Times*, 28.

Kaminer, W. (1998). The trouble with single sex schools. *The Atlantic Monthly*. http://www.theatlantic.com/doc/prem/199804/single-sex. Retrieved June 5, 2006.

Kleinfeld, J. (1999). Student performance: Males versus females. *The Public Interest, 134*, 3–20.

Lee, L., & Bryk, A. S. (1986). Effects of single sex schools on student achievement and attitudes. *Journal of Educational Psychology, 78*, 381–395.

Murphy, P., & Ivinson, G. (2000) *Construction of knowledge, social identities, and pedagogy in single and mixed sex groupings.* Paper presented at the annual meeting of the American Educational Research Association, New Orleans, LA.

NASSPE (2006). National Association for Single Sex Public Education. www.singlesexschools.org.

No Child Left Behind Act. P. b L. No. 107–110, 115 Stat. 1425, 5131 (a) (23), 107th Congress, 1st Session. *Congressional Record, 147* (7 June 2001), S5943-44 (statement of Hillary Clinton).

Rowe, K. J. (1988). Single sex and mixed sex classes: The effects of class type on student achievement, confidence and participation in mathematics. *Australian Journal of Education, 32*, 180–182.

Sadker, M., & Sadker, D. (1994). *Failing at fairness.* New York: Touchstone.

Sax, L. (2006, March 1). Single-sex: Separate but better? *Philadelphia Daily News.* http:// www.philly.com/mld.dailynews/news/opinion/13987331.htm. Retrieved June 15, 2006.

Shmurak, C. (1998). *Voice of hope. Adolescent girls at single sex and coeducational schools.* New York: Lang.

8

For Better or Worse
Classroom Dynamics in Single-Sex Science Classes

Karen B. Rogers

SINGLE-SEX VERSUS COEDUCATIONAL CLASSES IN MIDDLE SCHOOL MATHEMATICS AND SCIENCE

The 1970s ushered in a strong interest in gender-related differences, with perhaps the classic review of gender differences put forth by Maccoby and Jacklin (1974). From their work, which identified patterns of cognitive and academic differences among male and female learners, to the work of Fennema (1974) and Fennema and Sherman (1977), the research began to refocus more specifically on girls and their performance in mathematics and science. In the 3 decades since Maccoby and Jacklin, much study has looked at the psychosocial as well as the brain-related variables that influence or exaggerate gender differences among learners of varying abilities. As recently as 2001, Kerr and Cohn reported that the scales on gender study had tipped "in favor" of girls when considering the research studies reported in the past 2 decades. In this respect, the study reported in this chapter aims to expand beyond this focus to the impact of single-sex classes on both girls and boys.

In effect, there seem to have been two sets of explanations for the documented gender differences in performance on tests and in schools. One set of explanations seems to suggest that women's general abilities in mathematics and science are "restricted" by differences in the way their brains process and apprehend information. Benbow and Stanley (1984) contributed to this argument by attributing the higher mathematics scores of boys to endogenous factors rather than social ones, suggesting that females can't help but be inferior in mathematics and science due to lesser abilities in visualization and problem-solving skills.

The second set of explanations centers on the potential influence of differential environmental and sociocultural variables upon girls and boys. Those variables include, but are not limited to, parent expectations (Eccles, 1984; Rubin, Provenzano & Luria, 1974), teacher expectations (Cooley, Chauvin, & Karnes, 1984; Koehler, 1990), teacher perceptions of ability versus effort (Fennema, Peterson, Carpenter, & Lubinski, 1990), student perceptions of ability versus effort (Hollinger & Fleming, 1984; Kerr, 1995; Pintrich & Blumenfeld, 1985; Reis, 1998), representation of gender roles in texts and learning materials (Block, 1982; Peterson & Fennema, 1985), and community perceptions of gender-related expectations for achievement and performance (Renzulli & Reis, 1991). Although educators and researchers (e.g., Pallas & Alexander, 1983; Sadker & Sadker, 1994) since that time have argued strenuously for overcoming these deficiencies by increasing the encouragement of females to pursue advanced courses in these areas, the lack of representation of girls in math, science, and the technical fields of work continues to grow (American Association of University Women, 1992; Gavin, 1997; Henry & Manning, 1998).

Although there is an assumption that females and males receive an equal education when they are in the same classrooms, with the same teacher, using the same books (Benbow & Stanley, 1984), the assumption may be false, as circumstantial evidence uncovered in classroom studies suggests. Classroom activities are chosen more often to appeal to boys than to girls (Fennema & Peterson, 1987; Stallings, 1985). Boys receive more praise, a greater number of disciplinary contacts, and more general teacher-initiated contacts (Hall & Sandler, 1982; Sadker & Sadker, 1994). Teachers respond more often to boys' requests for help and criticize girls more frequently for the academic quality of their work (Webb & Kenderski, 1985). Even when overall sex differences are not found in patterns of interaction, a few male students often dominate teacher attention in mathematics classes (Sadker & Sadker, 1994). Kerr (1995) cited at least two education barriers that affect girls' achievement in science and mathematics classes: (1) boys are called upon three times more often than girls and receive more informative replies for their responses; and (2) male characters continue to dominate in science and mathematics textbooks. Likewise, girls tend to choose—and are allowed to choose—less demanding courses in those areas (Eccles, 1987).

Gender differences continue to prevail in self-efficacy, a quality reflected in measures of self-concept and course choice: Cramer and Oshima (1992), for example, concluded that girls continue to ascribe their difficulties in mathematics to a lack of ability, while boys attribute their difficulties to a lack of effort. At the same time, it is not clear that attribution differences are innate (Olszewski-Kubilius & Grant; 1996). Heller and Ziegler (1996), for example, have reported that retraining girls in attribution identification can result in enhanced performance for both boys and girls. Silverman (1993) asserted that "one factor that clearly undermines gifted adolescent girls' self-esteem is their belief that high ability means achieving good grades effortlessly" (p. 304). This may explain why they do not attribute success to effort.

Motivation to pursue mathematics or science as a career has been studied to some degree as well. There is some evidence that girls are more likely to choose a science career if their fathers are in science (Rejskind, Rapagna, & Gold, 1999). Dickens and Cornell (1993) reported that parents' own mathematical self-efficacy relates strongly to their expectations for their daughter's performance.

In studies of single-sex classes, Subotnik and Strauss (1995) reported that single-sex classes did not increase girls' participation in an advanced placement calculus class. Although Feldhusen and Willard-Holt (1993) noted that boys tended to ask more questions than girls, there is little evidence that teachers stop girls from calling out answers in class. Stone (1992) reported the common experience of educators and students in all-girls schools—they hold many advantages for girls: "At a single-sex school, the girls did not feel like second-class citizens, or fall silent in classroom discussions, or develop math anxiety, or settle for running for student government secretary" (p. 72). What is not so clear is the impact single-sex classes may have on boys. Is there an opposite picture for them when they find themselves surrounded by others of the same sex? In a small study by Reis and Kettle (1994), the researchers found that mixed groups in science resulted commonly in boys dominating and conducting the science activities, in comparison to single-sex girls' classes in which all girls fully participated.

Studies of actual performance have clearly demonstrated the differences of girls and boys in mathematics and science classes as well as on tests. Boys continue to score more highly on timed, competitive standardized tests of math and science, such as the Scholastic Aptitude Test (SAT; e.g., Halpern, 1989: Hyde & Fennema, 1990). Likewise, the more highly selective the sample of students analyzed in this research, the greater the differences in performance. When changes in time restrictions are made, however, the differences tend to decrease dramatically (Dreyden & Gallagher, 1989). Other research has found girls to be more accurate in math computation skills through middle school and to receive better grades in mathematics and science through high school (Kimball, 1989). In recognition of this difference in classroom performance, Kimball, among others, has argued that perhaps equal attention should be paid to classroom grades as the measure of actual learning in mathematics and science. Further, Reis (2002) has reported that girls are significantly less likely to major in mathematics or science in college, especially at the graduate level. Perhaps with a self-imposed perception that test scores equate with ability, coupled with fewer positive/encouraging interactions with teachers before reaching college levels (Rogers, 1990), the explanations for the significant "drop out" of highly able women from college and postgraduate studies in these fields are accounted for.

In the past few years, much has continued to be written about gender differences in mathematics and science among the gifted and talented (e.g., Arnold, Noble, & Subotnik, 1996; Ablard & Tissot, 1998; Siegle & Reis, 1998; Heller & Ziegler, 1996; Callahan, Cunningham, & Plucker, 1994). In many cases these writers have suggested that instructing gifted girls during the years of early adolescence in all-girls math and science classes might favorably influence attitudes toward the subjects as well as self-efficacy. Recent research on parochial schools suggests that single-sex classes do not affect girls' attitudes toward these two subjects as much as they do boys' attitudes. Ten years' study of single-sex selective high school achievement comparisons of boys and girls suggests this latter pattern as well. The purpose of this current study, therefore, was to determine what academic, motivational, instructional, and curricular benefits occur when gifted boys and girls are separated for instruction in math and science in a heterogeneous public middle school. It was hypothesized that the greatest differences would occur in instructional style, student motivation, and self-efficacy. It was also hypothesized that both boys and girls would benefit from the single-gender organization of instruction.

Questions continue to abound about the efficacy of single-sex classes. With that in mind, the purpose of this study was to compare the achievement, motivational, interactional, and self-esteem effects of single-sex and coeducational classes in science and mathematics among preadolescent girls and boys. The research question asked was *What are the effects of single-sex classes in public school mathematics and science on boys and girls of varying ability levels?* It was predicted, based on previous research, that

1. Placing gifted girls and boys in single-sex classes will improve math and science achievement.
2. Placing regular-ability girls and boys in single-sex classes will improve math and science achievement.
3. Placing gifted boys and girls in single-sex classes will improve self-efficacy and attitudes toward math, science, and learning.
4. Placing regular-ability girls and boys in single-sex classes will improve self-efficacy and attitudes toward math, science, and learning.
5. Teachers of single-sex classes will use different instructional management and delivery strategies for math and science instruction.

METHOD

Subjects

All 7th-grade students on a single suburban middle school team were included in the study. They were randomly assigned to class periods taught by one science teacher and one mathematics teacher. The 5th and 6th periods of the day were designated as the single-gender classes. During 5th period, the math teacher instructed an all-boys class while the science teacher worked with an all-girls class. For 6th period, the all-boys class went to the science teacher, while the math teacher instructed the all-girls group. Fourth-period classes, taught by these same two instructors, were randomly assigned mixed classes as the controls. In all, there were 51 boys and 55 girls involved in the four class groups (mixed science class, mixed math class, single-sex boys' science/math class, and single-sex girls' science/math class), of whom 55 were controls and 51 were the treatment classes. Nineteen students assigned to the four periods were formally identified as gifted. Over the course of the study, 7 students dropped from it due to moves from the school to other schools. Four were students in the single-sex classes and three were in the control groups.

Both teachers, willing volunteers to undertake the experiment, were female teachers with 12 and 15 years' experience in teaching their subject areas. The science teacher had initiated the project and had a particular interest in the concept of all-girls classes in science, while the mathematics teacher was interested in the impact of single-sex composition on boys.

Instrumentation

In this data-rich study, two instruments were developed for systematic perceptual and behavioral data collection. A questionnaire, "All About You," was developed to measure each participant's attitudes toward mathematics, attitudes toward science, cognitive styles and learning preferences, and general attitudes toward school and learning. Comprised of four sections, each assessing a construct of this motivation measure, the following constructs were included via statements relative to each construct being rated by students on a 5-point likert scale—Very true of me (5) to Very untrue of me (1). Section 1, which measured motivation for science and mathematics, clustered on five motivational constructs: (a) motivation and liking for the subject, (b) academic self-concept in science and mathematics based on performance, (c) academic self-concept based on opinions of others, (d) sense of control over performance, and (e) self-efficacy, mastery in science and mathematics. Section 2 measured motivation for school and learning, based upon (a) motivation for schooling, (b) academic self-concept based on performance, (c) academic self-concept based on reference, (d) sense of control over performances at school, and (e) perception of instructional mastery. Section 3 was adapted from Renzulli and Smith's (1974) Learning Style Inventory, eliciting ranked preferences for 8 categories of instructional delivery: projects, independent study, lecture, drill and recitation, programmed instruction, peer teaching, discussion, and games and simulations. Section 4 focused on student perceptions of their cognitive style and included the constructs of visual modality, auditory modality, tactile modality, kinesthetic modality, elaboration, independence, need for variety, and persistence. The questionnaire included 20 items on school and learning motivation, 19 items on attitude and self-efficacy in math, 20 items on attitude and self-efficacy in science, and 16 items on cognitive style and learning preference.

The second instrument was developed after a series of intense and indepth classroom observations of both single-sex and mixed math and science classes. Two observers remained in these classrooms over the period of 3 days, using the continuous narrative technique to characterize "typical" classroom behavior. From these narratives, an observation instrument, "Observation Summary," was developed that used the following protocol in subsequent applications to categorize and characterize each videotaped classroom period. Three main activities for each day were observed. For each, counts of individual behaviors and an assessment of the level of activity were made (high activity was indicated by 8 or more instances of student or teacher behavior, moderate activity ranged from 3 to 7 instances of that behavior, and low activity was judged for 0 to 2 instances of a behavior. The behaviors counted and assessed included

- Teacher talk/questions to individuals
- Students volunteering answers
- Noise level (instances of loud levels were counted)
- Energy level (high energy output counts)
- Teacher reminders to settle down, be quiet, get to work
- On-task student questions/comments
- Off-task student questions/comments
- Nonparticipatory student behavior
- Out-of-desk on-task student behavior
- Out-of-desk off-task student behavior
- Student-to-student negative comments
- Student self-criticism
- Competition for teacher's attention
- Competition for grades/marks
- Competition for peer recognition

Additionally, the number of boys and/or girls engaged in each of these behaviors, except the first four, was counted. An estimate of the percentage of time spent with each instance of the teacher talking to the class was made, as well as an estimate of the percentage of time spent in student-initiated questions or comments. With the use of this observation instrument with each videotaped class, possible intervening variables that might have affected that day's counts and ratings were noted, as well as any anecdotes, personal impressions, and comparisons seen on the tape.

In addition to these two instruments, the students' end-of-year science and math grades as well as their grades at the midyear and end of grade 7 in these two subjects were collected. Both the science teacher and her single-sex girls' and boys' classes wrote weekly journal entries, responding to a stimulus she provided. Small single-sex focus groups were conducted using a series of five questions once the semester was completed, and the teachers were interviewed in-depth about (a) their impressions of their teaching behaviors in each class setting, (b) perceived outcomes of the project, (c) preferences for class composition type, and (d) perceptions of student change by class composition type.

Procedure

Parents' permission for participation in the single-sex classes was obtained before school in grade 7 began. During the first week of class, students' attitudes and self-efficacy toward math and science were assessed using the "All About You" questionnaire for the randomly selected mixed-class periods in science and math, respectively, and for the single-sex class periods. Over the course of the semester, a camcorder placed in each teacher's classroom ran for the entire class period in both the mixed and single-sex classes for a minimum of 2 days per week; in addition, a complete recording of each day for the second week and next-to-last week of the semester in the four classes was run. The two teachers decided on which days to record and then all three of their respective classes were recorded on those designated afternoons. Days on which new concepts or content were being taught, discussions were being encouraged, or review of concepts learned was being conducted were the days these teachers targeted. An observational checklist was developed after several on-site visits by the researcher and research associate to measure the degree of student interaction with other students and with the teacher, focus and time on task, indicators of student "interest" in what was being taught, and to look for differences in the instructors' modes of instructing and presenting. The two observers, using this checklist independently, rated each videotape.

At the end of the semester, students' attitudes toward math and science and self-efficacy were again measured using the attitudinal scale. Students' grades and available achievement test scores in math and science from the prior year were compared to the end of the semester's performance. The two teachers were interviewed in depth to identify (1) differences they found among the classes, (2) the ways they taught and used instructional time, and (3) their own learning preferences. In addition, the science teacher asked students in both her mixed- and single-sex classes to journal several times over the semester about their reflections on class activities and classmates. These entries were content-analyzed by the lead researcher. For all the data collected, separate analyses were conducted on the district-identified gifted students in addition to analyses of all the students participating from this one 7th-grade team at the school.

End-of-the-year grades and data from a third administration of the "All About You" questionnaire were collected to register possible longer-term growth and change. The single-sex students were again interviewed as single-sex focus groups and the two teachers were also interviewed again in order for participants to reflect on comparisons of both classroom composition conditions.

RESULTS

The major findings partially supported all hypotheses of this study.

For both science and mathematics, single-gender classes tended to be more student-to-student and student-to-teacher interactive, more high energy, and more participative than mixed-gender classes. Distinct differences in instructional approach to mixed-gender and single-gender classes were found for both teachers. Both teachers tended to be more interactive with a wider group of students in the single-gender classes, and students themselves were much more interactive with both the teacher and classmates in those classes.

From the twice-weekly videotapes and the 2 full-week videotapes, counts of student-to-student and student-to-teacher interactions were significantly greater in both single-sex classes in both subject areas. For the single-sex girls' classes in science and mathematics, the students tended to work collaboratively with each other to help those who "didn't get" the tasks given. At some time in the semester, they had decided as a class to try to work a week ahead of the teacher's schedule in the science class in particular, so that by Tuesday of the week for which the task was to be completed, they would all be "free" to carry on more wide-ranging discussions about the implications of what they were learning. This indeed was what occurred for these girls: Many of the brighter ones would come in on Monday of the designated task week and then circulate before the formal start of class to survey who hadn't gotten the work done or didn't understand it. Then those who had completed the tasks would work with the noncompleters, while the teacher basically stood at the sidelines. For mathematics, this did not occur, but the girls tended to direct the teacher's instruction by asking pertinent questions about how to do things on a whole-group basis, and then those who did understand circulated to help those who had not mastered the concepts and skills yet. Very little direct instruction was provided by the two teachers in the single-sex girls' classes—less than one-quarter of the time in which these teachers "presented" in the mixed classes.

For the single-sex boys' classes, the teachers also did significantly less direct instruction, again about one-quarter of the actual time allocated in the mixed classes. The nature of interaction in these boys' classes, however, was significantly different than in the single-sex girls' classes. The boys vocally "protested" if the teacher wished to provide instructions and explanations. There were vocal comments, such as "Just let us get on with it and we will ask questions if we have any." The teacher complied and spent the majority of class time circulating among desks, helping the boys individually. Of issue, particularly in the mathematics class, was the boys' tendency, almost to a person, to denigrate those in the class who "didn't get it." It is suspected this resulted, in part, from the insistence on the group's part to each work on their own and receive individual help rather than work as a whole group. Differences in student-to-teacher interactions were also seen in the geographical distance maintained by both parties in the two single-sex classes. When the girls were working independently or collaboratively, they would go to the teacher when help was needed. For the boys, however, the teacher was "expected" to come to them.

Interviews of the two teachers at the conclusion of the study revealed some, but only slight, realization that they had actually related to the genders in very different ways. The two teachers were able to perceive that they were less "teachers" and more "facilitators" in the single-sex classes than they were in the mixed classes, but they hadn't fully realized how differently they and the students approached each other in the single-sex settings. The math teacher reported that in the single-sex boys' class there was little task involvement on the part of the boys and frequent veering off the topic, through tangential subjects brought up or rowdy behavior. She felt she had difficulty controlling this group. She reported that the boys had difficulty helping each other, did not want to hear her explanations, and spent considerable time making it difficult for her "to teach." She reported that she felt the boys had enjoyed the class but were reluctant to admit it in front of the other boys.

For the single-sex girls' math class, the teacher reported that the girls were her highest-achieving class of the day. They exhibited high competitive levels, but they spontaneously helped those who lagged behind and they were task oriented and ego involved.

For the three class composition types in science, similar findings were observed. The teacher reported her mixed class as "very malleable," passive in nature, and the easiest class to teach. The students "did what they were told to do." In contrast, the science teacher reported that her single-sex boys' group needed much more "nurturing" and were generally respectful and calm, but when they did get rowdy, she was easily able to get them back under control. She reported that the boys in this class worked well in groups or pairs and seemed anxious to get their work done in class so there would be no homework. She felt this group was not "very sharp" in science, but wanted to "best" the girls, so they tried very hard to do well. Although she reported many attempts to get her off task, she felt she was able to control this. The single-sex girls' class was described by the science teacher as her highest achieving and most competitive class. The girls tended to pair off spontaneously to help those who were struggling, in high/low pairs. The girls came prepared for class, did all the assignments and reviews she assigned for homework, and then spent class exploring further science issues as well as personal issues.

When asked which class conformation they preferred, both teachers reported they "felt more like the teacher" in the mixed classes and were "out of control" in the single-sex settings. They also reported feeling "more re-laxed" with the mixed classes, which were described as cooperative, task-focused, and focused on work completion rather than peer interaction.

Videotape observations did not corroborate any true lack of control in the single-sex settings, however; a more likely explanation for the differences in behavior may have been that they took their cues from the demonstrated preferences and expressed needs of each of their classes. Their approach, therefore, seemed more "alien" to their regular way of doing things when teaching in the single-sex classes. In all instances of mixed classes, the teachers did exhibit gender-fair behaviors, but in general the girls were less likely to answer and dominate in class. They tended to "follow the rules" for asking and answering questions in whole-group discussions. The mixed classes also tended to be run as lecture or whole-group discussion, with a strong emphasis on auditory learning. The mathematics teacher's perceptions of her single-sex boys' class was corroborated in that the boys were much more physically active, had higher noise levels, and were less truly "on task" than any of the other classes. The teacher with this math group tended to use more visual approaches to presentations and spent more time on pair and one-to-one interactions with students than in whole-group presentations. She traveled into the boys' individual spaces to do this.

The videotapes of the single-sex girls' math class showed students who exhibited high levels of energy and activity, were task involved, and whose noise levels were moderate. The teacher's manner in this class was more serious than in her other two classes, and students were more serious about doing well. There was a strong focus on auditory approaches, discussion, and small-group work. There were few one-on-one interactions. The girls tended to come into the teacher's space for help. The girls were consistently assertive about what they needed to know and were "out of their shells" in terms of showing the behaviors of active learning, as compared to the girls in the mixed class.

Videotape analyses of the mixed science class showed little to no cooperative work that crossed gender lines. The girls tended to "shepherd" good behavior by asking *how* questions and quieting the class down spontaneously. The teacher showed a good blend of visual and auditory teaching styles. Students tended to engage in more drill and practice and direct work on homework assignments in class, and much less time was spent on study or review outside of class time than for the two single-sex science classes. The single-sex boys' class showed an emphasis by the teacher on auditory learning with low noise levels and moderate physical activity and off-task behavior. The single-sex girls' class showed a "swarming" around the teacher in almost every observation period, taking over her responsibilities, interacting frequently with each other during class, and using across-the-group discussion on related science topics and the teacher's personal life. There was openness when they did not understand something. There seemed to be little evidence of boredom. The teacher's style in this composition type was primarily auditory. There were high noise and physical activity levels, but the class was never out of control during any observation. There seemed to be a strong sense of camaraderie among the girls, as evidenced by their complimentary remarks to each other, support for each other's ideas, and the relating that was done in almost every discussion conducted during the semester.

When asked which of the single-sex classes was preferable as a second choice of setting, the teachers did report a difference in their own attitudes about the two kinds of class mixes they were teaching: The math teacher felt most comfortable with the all-boys class and felt she did her better work there, while the science teacher preferred the all-girls class permutation.

Boys reported a preference for mixed-gender classes and stated that they were "punished" by being in an all-boys class. The girls in the single-sex class reported a preference for the all-girls classes.

From the first videotapings of the classes, the boys in the single-sex setting staged vocal protests about their "having to be" in the all-boys situation. They felt this was being done because the girls "needed" it and that it was not fair to them. In a later focus group with the boys, similar opinions were raised among each of the students participating. While in the single-sex settings, the boys spent much time concerned about "how far ahead" the girls were getting because they were getting to work with each other, and again the general classroom expression was that it was not fair to the boys.

When queried through individual journal writing for science, however, these same boys tended to be less negative about the single-sex situation. All 5 of the formally identified gifted students in the single-sex boys' class as well as 7 of the 21 regular students made brief remarks that led one to believe being separated by gender was not so bad. The single-sex boys' response showed that 4 were basically positive about their placement, 5 were very negative, and 17 had mixed feelings. The single-sex girls' class showed 22 positive responses, 1 negative one, and 7 with mixed feelings. For the mixed-class girls who responded with journal entries, 7 were positive about the idea of single-sex girls' classes and 7 had mixed feelings, while for the mixed-class boys, 5 were negative about the idea of single-sex boys' classes and 3 had mixed feelings. For the girls, the responses to single-sex placement were overwhelmingly positive, creating for them a feeling of safety and companionship, as well as a certain empowerment to succeed in the two subjects. Competition was stronger than in mixed classes, but it was inner directed, not "against" other girls in the group.

There seemed to be a large discrepancy between what the boys said aloud in interviews and on videotape and what they wrote about science classes in their journals. They were more positive when other boys did not hear what they had to say and only the teacher (and researchers) knew their true opinions. The gifted boys elaborated on having to do more of the work themselves and that this was probably good for them, and said that they were less distracted with the girls not present. Likewise, mention was made that they felt they were being more active learners in the single-sex class, whereas in mixed classes the girls always "made up" for any lack of preparation on their part. Two mentions were made of feeling that not knowing how well the girls were doing made them work a little harder to achieve than they might have with the girls actually in their classes. The focus group reiterated much of these individualized journal writings. Three "reasons" were given for wanting girls in their classes: (1) the girls look better than a class of just boys, (2) the girls make them behave more appropriately and with more civility, and (3) the girls always had the homework and the "right" answers so the teachers did not come down so hard on them (the boys) personally. This certainly begs the question of the value of mixed classes for optimal achievement of both genders!

No significant changes in self-efficacy or motivation toward learning and school were found for either treatment or control groups, but somewhat more positive attitudes toward math and science were found for the treatment groups.

For the five constructs contained in the "Motivation for School and Learning" questionnaire, administered pre- and posttreatment, two constructs (instructional mastery and motivation for school) showed no significant differences among the mixed and single-sex groups or across the time of the treatment. Three constructs, however, showed substantial differences pre- and posttest for some of the groups. Table 1 summarizes these mean responses. As can be seen, performance-based academic self-concept declined by midyear, regardless of class composition and ability level. Gifted students, regardless of class composition participation, reported higher levels of this form of self-concept than all other learners. Of some concern was the significant drop of academic self-concept for special education learners across the year. At the beginning of the year, there was no pattern of consistent difference in motivational levels between the mixed- and single-sex classes or in the size of the decline at the post measure, and there was a slight upturn in the final measurement, except for one item: "Teachers count on me for correct answers." The single-sex class students reported a significantly greater decline in this perception than did those students in the mixed settings. This may corroborate with the actual changes of behavior observed in the teachers in their interactions in class.

In their motivation for science and mathematics, somewhat similar patterns of movement were found, but only for a very few items among the 34 represented across the science and mathematics attitude statements contained in the questionnaires. As table 2 summarizes, a decline in viewing labs and experiments as the most interesting aspect of science changed significantly for the single-sex group as well as gifted students in both class composition permutations. Focus group follow-ups brought forth the idea that students in the single-sex groups found more satisfaction than in previous years in the discussion of implications/application aspect of science. A similar phenomenon was found for the single-sex, regular ability, special education, and gifted groups for perceiving puzzlers and extra problems as a very positive aspect of math learning. Again, through focus group probes, the discussion and application aspects of mathematics in the single-sex composition settings seemed the major reason for this change. Gender stereotypes about math capability seemed to loom larger among ability-related analyses than for class composition, although all groups came to feel less strongly that this "sometimes statement" was true over the course of the year. In doing one's best on work in science and mathematics, all groups declined by midyear, but of some concern is the greater degree of decline for special education students.

Table 1. Pre/Post Difference in Attitudes toward School and Learning

Construct and Statement	Mixed-Gender Mean	Single-Gender Mean	Gifted Mean	Regular Mean	Special Education Mean
Academic Self-Concept— Performance Based	True	True	Very True	True	True
"I am happy with my schoolwork."					
• Pre-Measure	3.05	3.14	3.52	3.00	2.81
• Post-Measure	2.82*	2.83*	2.95*	2.79*	2.10*
• Final Measure	2.90	3.01	3.22	2.99	2.21
"I am satisfied with my grades."					
• Pre-Measure	3.12	3.29	3.52	3.12	2.96
• Post-Measure	2.64*	2.73*	3.00*	2.65*	2.30**
• Final Measure	2.69	2.82	3.45	2.75	2.22
"I am proud of the work I do at school."					
• Pre-Measure	3.20	3.14	3.52	3.15	2.81
• Post-Measure	2.78*	2.75*	3.10**	2.77**	2.20**
• Final Measure	2.81	2.66	3.32*	2.70	2.15
Academic Self-Concept— Reference Based	True/ Sometimes True	True/ Sometimes True	True	True/ Sometimes True	True/ Not True
"I take pride in things I hear about my schoolwork."					
• Pre-Measure	3.02	2.90	3.24	2.90	2.85
• Post-Measure	2.84*	2.58*	3.15	2.72*	1.70***
• Final Measure	2.80	2.66	3.20	2.69	1.58
"Teachers count on me for the correct answers."					
• Pre-Measure	2.47	2.38	2.48	2.39	2.54
• Post-Measure	2.28*	2.04*	2.42	2.20*	1.60***
• Final Measure	2.32	2.30	2.50	2.19	1.50
Sense of Control Over Performance Sometimes True	True/ Sometimes True	True/ Sometimes True	True/ Sometimes True	True/ Sometimes True	True/ Not True
"I check my work before handing it in."					
• Pre-Measure	2.67	2.63	2.81	2.62	2.62
• Post-Measure	2.20**	2.19**	2.35**	2.22**	1.80***
• Final Measure	2.40*	2.35*	2.60*	2.39*	1.79
"I keep trying to improve my school skills."			(Very True)		(True)
• Pre-Measure	3.30	3.39	3.67	3.33	2.92
• Post-Measure	2.96*	3.08*	3.00**	3.06*	2.90
• Final Measure	3.19	3.29*	3.51**	3.22	2.99
"I can get good grades if I work hard."	(Very True)	(Very True)	(Very True)	(Very True)	(Very True)
• Pre-Measure	3.75	3.78	3.71	3.79	3.69
• Post-Measure	3.54*	3.58*	3.70	3.55*	3.40*
• Final Measure	3.55	3.90	3.69	3.62	3.30

*p" .05; **p" .01; ***p" .001
Mean Ranges: 1.00–1.66 not true; 1.67–2.50 sometimes true; 2.51–3.33 true; 3.34–4.00 very true

Table 2. Pre/Post Mean Differences in Attitudes toward Mathematics and Science

Construct and Statement	Mixed-Gender Mean	Single-Gender Mean	Gifted Mean	Regular Mean	Special Education Mean
Motivation/ Liking for the Subject	True	True	Very True/ True	True	True
"Labs and experiments are the most interesting part of science."					
• Pre-Measure	3.31	3.25	3.52	3.20	3.38
• Post-Measure	3.24	2.88**	3.20*	3.05*	3.10*
• Final Measure	3.15	2.95	3.33	3.12	2.97
"I like puzzlers, extra problems that use math."	(True/ Sometimes True)	(True/ Sometimes True)	(True/ Sometimes True)	(True/ Sometimes True)	(True/ Sometimes True)
• Pre-Measure	2.68	2.82	3.10	2.58	2.92
• Post-Measure	2.08*	2.19**	2.30**	2.09**	2.00**
• Final-Measure	2.10	2.03	2.54*	2.10	2.11
Academic Self-Concept in Subject–Performance	Sometimes True	Sometimes True	Sometimes True/ Not True	Sometimes True	Sometimes True
"Girls are better than boys at mathematics."					
• Pre-Measure	1.96	1.91	1.93	1.95	1.92
• Post-Measure	1.65*	1.63*	1.47**	1.77*	1.20**
• Final Measure	1.60	1.71	1.56	1.80	1.34
Sense of Control Over Performance in Subject	True	True	True	True	True/ ST
"I try to do my best on math tasks."					
• Pre-Measure	3.34	3.30	3.38	3.35	3.31
• Post-Measure	3.00*	3.02*	3.20*	3.08*	2.40***
• Final Measure	2.98	3.15	3.28	3.16	2.30

*p ″ .05; **p ″ .01; ***p ″ .001*
Mean Ranges: 1.00–1.66 not true; 1.67–2.50 sometimes true; 2.51–3.33 true; 3.34–4.00 very true

An analysis of changes in gifted students' attitudes toward mathematics and science was conducted, according to the funding support provided for this study. The comparative changes in attitude toward mathematics between single-sex and mixed participation can be seen in table 3 and changes for science in table 4. As can be seen in table 3, the single-sex and mixed gifted students had significantly different perceptions on 15 of the 20 items, but even more interesting are the significant changes in attitude that occurred according to their class composition participation. Except for 3 items, the single-sex class gifted students improved in their attitudes toward mathematics significantly. Their attitudes remained constant for math requiring hard work and trying to do their best work in math, while the perception that boys get more attention in math classes declined in strength. For the mixed group, there were fewer significant changes in attitude, and for 8 items the attitude declined. Attitudes for the regular students paralleled the general mean differences reported in table 2.

As can be seen in table 4, the single-sex and mixed gifted students had significantly different perceptions of science on 12 of the 20 items, but even more interesting are the significant changes in attitude that occurred according to their class composition participation. Of the 13 items that showed significant change across the school year, the single-sex gifted students significantly improved in their attitudes toward science on 9 of the items and declined more significantly on 3 items. Their attitudes remained constant for perceiving they were good at science, feeling science is their favorite subject, enjoying the new ideas in learning science, finding science easy, visiting science museums, and feeling that girls are better at science than boys. For the mixed gifted group, there were fewer significant changes in attitude. Interestingly, both the single-sex and mixed gifted students came to believe boys try to take over in science classes, but this feeling was considerably stronger for the single-sex respondents. Attitudes for the regular students paralleled the general mean differences reported in table 2.

The learning preferences and cognitive styles of these students tended to change significantly across the study in two primary areas: preference for discussion and independent learning.

Among the 16 cognitive styles and learning preferences surveyed among the children, analyses of ability-related and class composition–related differences in preference showed significant differences for four items. As table 5 illustrates, there were declines for all groups between the beginning and end of the first semester, but significant gains in the preference for discussion for the single-sex group by the end of the year. The special education group, however, declined in their preference for discussion consistently and significantly throughout the year. For independent study as a preference for learning, the gifted students, regardless of class composition, came to change significantly more to the positive as the year progressed. Special education students began the year believing in the efficacy of the visual medium more strongly than all other groups but came to agree with the regular students about it as a preference as the year progressed.

Table 3. Gifted Students' Mean Math Attitudes by Class Composition Participation

Statement	Single-Sex Pre-Test Mean	Int.	Single-Sex Post-Test Mean	Int.	Mixed Pre-Test Mean	Int.	Mixed Post-Test Mean	Int.
Math is favorite subject	2.00	ST	2.87*	T	2.91	T	2.60*	T
Best teachers are in math	2.20	ST	2.63*	T	2.36	ST	3.10*	T
Must work hard to do well in math	3.50	VT	3.50	VT	3.54	VT	3.20*	T
Am very good in math	2.50	ST	3.37**	VT	3.18	T	2.90*	T
Plan to study more math in school	2.40	ST	3.25**	T	3.00	T	3.20	T
New ideas in math are favorite part	2.40	ST	3.13**	T	2.63	T	2.70	T
Math explorations are favorite part	2.10	ST	3.00**	T	2.91	T	2.40*	ST
Love doing puzzlers, extra problems	2.20	ST	3.00**	T	2.63	T	2.70	T
Learn math outside of school	1.80	ST	2.50*	ST	2.45	ST	2.40	ST
Math is easy for me	1.80	ST	3.37***	VT	2.70	T	2.80	T
Try to do best work in math	2.80	T	2.75	T	3.18	T	3.20	T
Watch TV programs about math	1.00	NT	2.28**	ST	1.90	ST	1.80	ST
Visit exhibits about math outside school	1.60	NT	2.71**	T	2.54	T	2.20	ST
Want a math career	1.30	NT	3.00***	T	2.27	ST	1.80*	ST
Want more math classes daily	1.00	NT	2.25**	ST	2.27	ST	1.80*	ST
Boys get most attention in math	1.87	ST	1.40*	NT	1.50	ST	1.87*	ST
Girls are better in math than boys	1.60	NT	2.00*	ST	1.90	ST	2.00	ST
Boys take over in math classes	1.30	NT	2.13**	ST	1.90	ST	1.70	ST
Can learn anything in math if I work hard	3.20	T	3.75**	VT	3.88	VT	3.50*	VT
Want longer math periods	1.70	ST	2.75**	T	2.36	ST	2.30	ST

*p ≤ .05; **p ≤ .01; ***p ≤ .001

Mean Ranges: 1.00–1.66 not true; 1.67–2.50 sometimes true; 2.51–3.33 true; 3.34–4.00 very true

Interpretations: NT not true; ST sometimes true; T true; VT very true

Table 4. Gifted Students' Mean Science Attitudes by Class Composition Participation

Statement	Single-Sex Pre-Test Mean	Int.	Single-Sex Post-Test Mean	Int.	Mixed Pre-Test Mean	Int.	Mixed Post-Test Mean	Int.
Science is favorite subject	2.30	ST	2.38	ST	1.80	SR	1.90	ST
Best teachers are in science	3.60	VT	2.13	ST	2.00	ST	2.00	ST
Must work hard to do well in science	2.10	ST	3.50***	VT	3.60	VT	3.30*	T
Am very good in science	2.70	T	3.00	T	2.36	ST	2.70*	T
Plan to study more science in school	2.40	ST	2.88*	T	2.45	ST	2.20	ST
New ideas in science are favorite part	2.50	ST	2.75	T	2.45	ST	2.40	ST
Science labs, experiments are favorite part	3.10	T	3.25	T	3.45	VT	3.90*	VT
Love to read about science	1.50	NT	2.38**	ST	1.91	ST	1.90	ST
Learn science outside of school	1.80	ST	2.38**	ST	2.09	ST	2.10	ST
Science is easy for me	2.70	T	2.88	T	2.40	ST	2.30	ST
Try to do best work in science	3.50	VT	2.63**	T	3.36	VT	3.10	T
Watch TV programs about science	1.80	ST	2.13**	ST	2.18	ST	2.10	ST
Visit science museums outside school	2.50	ST	2.63	T	2.72	T	2.70	T
Would like to be scientist	1.90	ST	2.50**	ST	1.72	ST	1.80	ST
Want more science classes daily	1.80	ST	1.50*	NT	1.60	NT	1.10**	NT
Boys get most attention in science	1.40	NT	1.75	ST	1.63	NT	1.60	NT
Girls are better in science than boys	1.80	ST	1.88	ST	1.30	NT	1.40	NT
Boys take over in science classes	1.50	NT	3.88***	VT	1.45	NT	3.30***	T
Can learn anything in science if I work hard	3.20	T	2.00***	ST	3.00	T	2.40**	ST
Want longer science periods	2.20	ST	4.00***	VT	1.80	ST	3.90***	VT

* $p \leq .05$; ** $p \leq .01$; *** $p \leq .001$

Mean Ranges: 1.00–1.66 not true; 1.67–2.50 sometimes true; 2.51–3.33 true; 3.34–4.00 very true

Interpretations: NT not true; ST sometimes true; T true; VT very true

Significant differences in academic achievement were found for the treatment group, gifted students, and special education students over the course of the year, when compared with their previous grades.

The students' previous science grades at the end of 6th grade were the baseline for measuring achievement changes in the study. As table 6 shows, there were declines in science marks for the two quarters over which this study extended for all groups except regular and special education students, but as the year progressed the grades began to improve

Table 5. Mean Cognitive Style Differences by Ability Level and Class Composition

Style	Mixed Mean	Single-sex Mean	Gifted Mean	Regular Mean	Special Educ. Mean
Discussion	True	True	True	True	True
"I like discussing materials with other students."					
• Pre-Measure	2.80	2.90	2.62	2.90	3.25
• Post-Measure	2.68 *	2.63 *	2.75	2.63 *	1.78 ***
• Final Measure	2.77	3.12 **	2.89	2.71	1.50 *
"I learn through discussion."					
• Pre-Measure	3.11	3.00	3.19	3.32	3.00
• Post-Measure	2.82 *	2.79 *	2.90 *	2.82 **	2.70 *
• Final Measure	2.80	2.95 *	3.01	2.90	2.60
Independent Study	True	True	True/ Very True	True	True/Sometimes True
"I love to work alone on my own topic of interest."					
• Pre-Measure	2.84	2.82	2.76	2.82	2.89
• Post-Measure	2.48 **	2.33 **	3.00 *	2.33 **	2.56 *
• Final Measure	2.61	2.43	3.57 **	2.55 *	2.41
Visual Modality	True	True	True	True	True
"I need to see something done to learn."					
• Pre-Measure	2.64	2.62	2.74	2.53	3.00
• Post-Measure	2.69	2.77 *	2.65	2.75 *	2.70 *
• Final Measure	2.77	2.68	2.66	2.81	2.81

* $p \leq .05$; **$p \leq .01$; ***$p \leq .001$
Mean Ranges: 1.00–1.66 not true; 1.67–2.50 sometimes true; 2.51–3.33 true; 3.34–4.00 very true

Table 6. Mean Pre/Post Differences in Mathematics and Science Achievement

Subject	Mixed Mean	Single-sex Mean	Gifted Mean	Regular Mean	Special Educ. Mean
Science Grades					
Quarter 1	7.66	7.84	11.30	7.88	4.01
Quarter 2	5.68 *	5.82 *	8.67 **	8.01	4.55
Quarter 3	6.03	6.15	9.02	7.00 *	3.25 *
Quarter 4	7.63 *	8.33 *	10.99 *	7.45	5.53 *
Mathematics Grades					
Quarter 1	5.88	5.66	10.13	4.57	3.49
Quarter 2	6.83	6.61	9.96	6.56	6.52 **
Quarter 3	7.54	8.12 *	10.42	6.88	6.19
Quarter 4	8.42 *	9.12 *	11.12	8.34 **	6.15

$* p \leq .05; ** p \leq .01$
Grades: A = 12, A- = 11, B+ = 10, B = 9, B- = 8, C+ = 7, C = 6, C- = 5, D+ = 4, D = 3, D- = 2, F = 0

almost to the beginning point of the previous year. Special education students and the single-sex students as a whole surpassed their previous performances in science substantially. In mathematics, grades went up substantially in each succeeding quarter of the year, with the greatest gains registered by the single-sex group, regular students, and special education students.

DISCUSSION

Five sets of findings were discovered in this data-rich, multimethods, quasi-experimental study. First, differences in the ways teachers taught and the ways students behaved in single-sex and mixed classes were found. More frequent student-teacher interactions, higher noise and energy levels, and more active learning were found for single-sex classes in both mathematics and science. Teachers did less "teaching" and more "discussing" or "facilitating" in the single-sex classes but reported feeling more "comfortable" teaching in the mixed settings. Explaining these differences is difficult. To begin with, the teachers seemed to take their cues from the verbal and nonverbal demands of each classroom of students — evidence, perhaps, of teaching effectiveness. But this resulted in substantial changes in teacher role and teacher interaction with students.

Teachers maintained their distance from most students in mixed settings, but were in closer proximity in the single-sex classes. However, the girls came to the teacher for this proximity, while the boys had the teacher come to them. Competition was much more in evidence in both single-sex classes, but it focused very differently by gender. Could it be that the safety and comfort the girls reported in the single-sex settings left them free to compete more with themselves and against themselves, while the boys in single-sex settings no longer perceived the "cover" of girls doing the work for them and competed against the girls' work ethic in trying to outdo them and denigrating each other's performances in the single-sex setting along the way? Or could it be that the social maturity and readiness of girls to cooperate and collaborate was best supported when they only had to manage their own gender, thus creating a healthy learning environment in science and math classes, while the boys, with less maturity, could not find the cooperative mode in order to improve their chances of "winning" the achievement game as they perceived it? Perhaps direct instruction in collaboration and cooperative learning would improve the boys' chances of feeling equally safe and comfortable in single-sex classes. Further research might be focused on answering these questions.

The second result showed that boys tended to prefer mixed settings, while the girls tended to prefer single-sex classes. Some of this has been discussed in the previous paragraphs. Despite this difference, however, boys were not so vociferous about negative perceptions of single-sex when they could express their views independently of the whole group. What is there about the learning climate that may have contributed to this set of perceptions? Did the boys truly feel girls are given more advantages by being allowed to learn without boys in the mix and did not want such dominance to prevail? What prompted the boys to feel unsafe, with self-efficacy "threatened" in the all-boys' situation, while the girls felt safe and comfortable? Was it merely the manner in which this experiment was structured—no previous explanations of what was being done or why it was being done and no opportunity for either gender to "choose" which setting they wanted, with boys reacting negatively to this lack of control or voice and girls "accepting" it as something they were already used to or could live with?

The third change found in this study showed no change in self-efficacy or motivation toward learning and school regardless of class setting over the course of the year, but considerable differences in motivation for and self-efficacy in math and science. There were significantly more positive attitudes toward both math and science for students in the single-sex classes by the end of the school year. In mathematics, students in the single-sex class who had returned to the mixed classroom in the second semester were significantly more positive about viewing math as their favorite subject, the math teacher as their favorite teacher, and liking all the "extra" aspects of math, such as puzzlers and new ideas. They tended to become more convinced that math is easy and that they would like more math classes and longer classes daily. They increased in their belief that they could learn anything in math if they just worked hard enough. Although none of these reflects directly on the dual composition experience the single-sex group had, one must wonder if the more active learning that occurred in the first semester of the year, subsequently compared with a return to a more traditional form of learning in the second semester, convinced them that they could learn in any environment. Perhaps the variety of math classes over the course of the year also convinced them that mathematics is doable and fun. Interestingly, the single-sex students, both boys and girls, jumped significantly in their belief that boys take over in math classes, but they did not feel so strongly as the mixed students that boys tend to get all the attention in math classes. Perhaps with the single-sex students "back" in the mixed classes, these latter students realized how differently the single-sex girls felt about the first semester and then took a look around. All students on the team were aware of what occurred when the first semester was over. All of the girls in the single-sex class signed a petition to be allowed to continue as a single-sex class, but administration was not in a position to allow it to happen. Sadly, when the next year came, the school did offer single-sex options in mathematics and science in addition to mixed classes. Forty-two girls signed up for single-sex classes, but only 9 boys did. Because there were not enough boys for a single-sex boys' class, the girls were not allowed to have one either.

Self-efficacy in and attitudes toward science showed distinct differences among the two composition types as well, but along different constructs. The students in the single-sex classes became more positive that if they worked hard they could do well in science. They reported that they were "good" at science, that they planned to study more science in the years to come, and that they would like to become scientists. One suspects that the teacher's more relaxed and sharing attitude in the single-sex classes may have led to these perceptions. Both single-sex classes, however, went down in their perception that their best teacher was in science. Perhaps being part of a semester in which they took an active part in their own learning without the traditional teaching led them to believe that less actual "teaching" was going on. These 7th-grade students may not view a teacher who is facilitating as truly "teaching." Although both class composition groups came to feel more strongly that boys get most of the attention and take over in science class, it was the single-sex students who jumped significantly in this belief over the course of the year. It might be suspected that with the girls having only themselves and the science teacher for a semester, they noticed the difference when they returned to the mixed setting. For the boys, who also came to feel so strongly about this, could it be the dominating sort of atmosphere that was created in both math and science caused them to reflect on this tendency in themselves? Or could it be that when they returned to the mixed setting they also saw how the domination by boys of activities and of teacher attention happened when girls were in the class?

That the learning preferences for discussion and independent learning changed significantly was also an interesting side note of this study. All groups had decided at the end of the first semester that discussion was not particularly pleasurable, but by the end of the year, the single-sex students opinions had risen significantly in "liking" to share ideas through discussion. Learning through discussion, however, was a different matter. None of the comparison groups felt more positively about this at the end of the year. Perhaps with a semester to discuss and a semester to learn by listening to lectures and doing assignments, the students came to see the pleasure of discussion but not the academic benefit of it as a learning tool. The gifted students became much more firmly convinced by year's end that they liked independent learning. That this is due to "too much" shared work in the single-sex and mixed classes might be a possible explanation. The liking of independent work went down significantly for the single-sex students. Perhaps because the boys had insisted on it in the first semester and had had the opportunity to learn that way, they decided they much preferred the mixed situation, with the girls sharing answers, to having to do it all themselves. For the single-sex girls, could it be that they had come to enjoy the freewheeling, sharing, and collaborative atmosphere of that first semester, such that they saw more pleasure at year's end in working together rather than alone?

Finally, there were significant differences in academic achievement in science and mathematics over the course of the year. At the end of the first semester, single-sex, mixed, and gifted students were down considerably in science, but their grades continued to rise through the next semester. The mixed and gifted students were almost up to their beginning achievement level by the end of the year. In the single-sex group, students were able to rise above their beginning level and were achieving significantly higher than were the mixed students. The regular and special education students in science went up at the end of the first quarter, then moved down considerably but began inching back up by the end of the year. It seems clear that all these students, new to the school itself, had to adjust to new systems of grading, but did pick up on the strategies needed to get their grades to acceptable levels. The shock of new school, new friends, and higher expectations had dissipated by year's end. Why the single-sex students would become more adept at this than the mixed students suggests some interesting possibilities. Could it be that they had learned how to be self-directed while working on assignments in science (for the girls, doing the work on weekends so class time could be used for discussion; for the boys, doing their work independently during class time, and this skill translated into better grades)? Or could it be that having practiced as active learners, even when they went back into the traditional setting, the habits of mind they acquired aided in higher achievement?

In mathematics four of the five comparison groups went up: mixed, single-sex, regular, and special education students. The gifted went down in the first quarter and then move steadily upward. Significant was the difference in end-of-year achievement between the mixed and single-sex students. Perhaps the same explanations discussed for science apply here as well. The single-sex students had learned how to become active learners and to work independently in an effective manner, and were better able to transfer this to the acquisition of math grades. Of great concern, however, were the special education students, who, after their first quarter, went down significantly for the remainder of the year. It seems evident that regardless of class composition, they were not receiving the instructional support they needed to achieve satisfactorily in middle school.

It is evident that both the boys and girls who participated in the single-sex math and science classes made some positive changes in their perceptions of math and science learning, the pleasures to be gained from these areas of study, and in their achievement in these subjects. These outcomes do seem to reflect positively on the experiences they enjoyed in the single-sex classes. That they became more active learners, became more independent in their accountability for achievement, and yet (for the girls) grew to enjoy collaboration and discussion of ideas more seem to be positive benefits of this kind of class composition. The reasons provided by the boys for why they preferred mixed settings do not seem beneficial enough for the girls to warrant putting their strong desire for single-sex classes aside. The single-sex girls, in particular, created a healthy, academically focused, cooperative learning environment in which most felt accepted by each other and in which they could be themselves. They took over the class reins from the teacher in an "active learning" sort of way, demonstrating a collaborative leadership rather than a competitive one. The single-sex boys had difficulty creating such an environment, perhaps because of a gap in their cooperative/social skills development. With direct instruction in cooperative learning, could this gap be remediated enough to make single-sex classes just as beneficial to them? Further study might try to answer this question.

In general, the gifted students in this study were not overly influenced by single-sex or mixed class placement; they stayed ahead across both class structures. For the general population of this sample, however, the single-sex students' achievement increased in both math and science. The gifted students' attitudes toward math and science were impacted by single-sex placement. Although they declined in ego-involved engagement, they increased in task-involved engagement. They thought less highly of their teachers, but increased in seeing their own future in science and math and in engaging in science and math learning outside of school. Perhaps as a result of more "voice" in their single-sex classrooms, they wanted more and longer school classes in these subjects. Furthermore, the single-sex classes in science and math for the girls seemed to free both the gifted and regular-ability learners to explore beyond the curriculum. They cooperated spontaneously to ensure that all students "mastered" the requirements, so that class time could be issues discussion time. It became "OK" to admit when something was not known and students could trust that there would be no put-downs.

Despite the interesting outcomes of this study, it is clear that there were many limitations. Only female teachers were used in the study. Future studies that use only male teachers under the same conditions would help determine if women only are likely to change their teaching styles when different circumstances demand it. Further study, too, on whether or not all-boys classes taught by a male teacher and all-girls classes taught by a female teacher influence the ultimate outcomes experienced here. Several students, especially the boys, were not happy that they had no choice of which class type they were placed in. Perhaps a study in which students might choose which permutation they are placed in would alter the outcomes in positive ways for the boys. The shortness of the treatment is also of concern here. A minimum of a full school year would have perhaps told a different story, or at least confirmed the beginnings of findings found in this one.

Finally, many of the outcomes in this study, especially those dealing with attitudes, are difficult to extricate from whether the declines were a typical "7th-grade slump" or whether the changes were directly related to single-sex versus mixed conditions. There was also difficulty in teasing out whether achievement and attitude levels of gifted students differed significantly as a result of single-sex versus mixed conditions. They seemed to react similarly to the general population in many of the outcomes measured in this study. Further research will need to look more closely at what actually occurs for them in both compositions. It may be that when the math and science curricula are not consciously differentiated, as was the case in this study, not much is going to happen for them, either achievement-wise or attitudinally, no matter what the class composition.

Of some benefit has been the development of a systematic method for analyzing extensive videotape data. The instrument, developed after numerous actual observations, worked well and showed good inter-rater reliability in the ultimate analysis of student and teacher classroom interactions. Likewise, this study is data-rich and represents a good collection of both quantitative and qualitative results to draw fuller pictures of the comparative classroom contexts. The teachers in this study used differential instructional management and delivery strategies for each class permutation, adapting to the "demands" of the students in these classes. The two teachers tended to see this as "adaptation" rather than "bias" toward one gender or the other. It would probably have not been so evident if a mixed-methods approach that involved observation, interview, and self-report had not been employed.

What this study has attempted is to explore what differences can occur for girls (and boys) in math and science by changing the learning environment. Recently, a furor was created by Harvard University president Lawrence Summers's January 2005 remarks that the "reason" there were fewer women in mathematical and scientific careers was that there are innate biological differences in brain development between males and females. Charles Murray (2005), a fellow at the American Enterprise Institute, editorialized, "If you were to query all the scholars who deal professionally with data about the cognitive repertoires of men and women, all but a fringe would accept that the sexes are different, and that genes are clearly implicated." Continuing his argument, Murray stated that knowing there are differences does not change the fact that "some women are terrific mathematicians" and that the truly important outcome of our recognition is that educators must do everything humanly possible to put the individual's abilities as their focus of attention rather than one's group membership to one sex or the other. What occurred for the boys and girls in this study did not break huge amounts of new ground, but it did focus on the learning environment and how that setting can hinder or enhance the abilities that are displayed within it. With relatively small changes in teacher behavior—allowing the students to take on a more active role in their own learning—gains were made in attitudes toward and self-efficacy in math and science, and accompanying rises in achievement in those areas was also an important outcome. Both boys and girls were able to bring out their best, regardless of their innate abilities designated by gender or motivation. It is hoped that future studies will replicate the modest results found here.

REFERENCES

Ablard, K. E., & Tissot, S. L. (1998). Young students' readiness for advanced mathematics: Precocious abstract reasoning. *Journal for the Education of the Gifted, 21*, 206–223.

Arnold, K., Noble, K. D., & Subotnik, R. F. (Eds.). (1996). *Remarkable women.* Cresskill, NJ: Hampton Press.

American Association of University Women. (1992). *The AAUW report: How schools shortchange girls*. Washington, DC: AAUW.

American Association of University Women. (1998). *Separated by sex: A critical look at single-sex education for girls*. Washington, DC: AAUW.

Benbow, C. P., & Stanley, J. C. (1984). Gender and the science major: A study of mathematically precocious youth. In M. W. Steinkamp & J. L. Maehr (Eds.), *Women in Science*. Greenwich, CT: JAI Press, 165–196.

Block, J. H. (1982). *Sex role identity and ego development*. San Francisco, CA: Jossey-Bass.

Callahan, C., Cunningham, C. M., & Plucker, J. A. (1994). Foundations for the future: The socio-emotional development of gifted adolescent women. *Roeper Review, 17*, 99–105.

Cooley, D., Chauvin, J., & Karnes, F. (1984). Gifted females: A comparison of attitudes by male and female teachers. *Roeper Review, 6*, 164–167.

Cramer, J., & Oshima, T. C. (1992). Do gifted females attribute their mathematics performance differently than other students? *Journal for the Education of the Gifted, 16*, 18–35.

Dickens, M. N., & Cornell, D. C. (1993). Parent influences on mathematics self-concept of high ability adolescent girls. *Journal for the Education of the Gifted, 17*, 53–73.

Dreyden, J. I., & Gallagher, S. A. (1989). The effects of time and direction changes on the SAT performance of academically talented adolescents. *Journal for the Education of the Gifted, 12*, 187–204.

Eccles, J. S. (1984). Sex differences in mathematics participation. In M. W. Steinkamp & M. L. Maehr (Eds.), *Advances in Motivation and Achievement* (pp. 93–137). Greenwich, CT: JAI Press.

Eccles, J. S. (1987). Gender roles and women's achievement-related decisions. *Psychology of Women Quarterly, 11*(2), 135–172.

Feldhusen, J. F., & Willard-Holt, C. (1993). Gender differences in classroom interaction and career aspirations of gifted students. *Contemporary Education Psychology, 18*, 355–362.

Fennema, E. (1974). Mathematics learning and the sexes: A review. *Journal for Research in Mathematics Education, 5*, 126–139.

Fennema, E., & Peterson, P. L. (1987). Effective teaching for girls and boys: The same or different? In D. Berliner & B . Rosenshine (Eds.), *Talks to teachers* (pp. 111–125). New York: Random House.

Fennema, E., Peterson, P. L., Carpenter, T. P., & Lubinski, C. A. (1990). Teachers' attributions and beliefs about girls, boys, and mathematics. *Educational Studies in Mathematics, 21*, 55–69.

Fennema, E., & Sherman, J. (1977). Sex-related differences in mathematics achievement, spatial visualization, and affective factors. *American Educational Research Journal, 14*, 51–71.

Gavin, M. K. (1997). A gender study of students with high mathematics ability: Personological, educational, and parental variables related to the intent to pursue quantitative fields of study. Unpublished doctoral dissertation. Storrs: University of Connecticut.

Hall, R., & Sandler, B. (1982). *The classroom climate: A chilly one for women.* Washington, DC: Project on the Status and Education of Women, Association of American Colleges.

Halpern, D. (1989). The disappearance of cognitive gender differences: What you see depends on where you look. *American Psychologist, 44*, 1156–1158.

Heller, K. A., & Ziegler, A. (1996). Gender differences in mathematics and the sciences: Can attribution retraining improve the performance of gifted females? *Gifted Child Quarterly, 40*, 200–210.

Henry, J., & Manning, G. (1998). *Gender-based intervention making computer science appealing to girls in high school.* Unpublished master's inquiry project, University of Connecticut, Storrs.

Hollinger, C. L., & Fleming, E. S. (1984). Internal barriers to the realization of potential: Correlates and interrelationships among gifted and talented female adolescents. *Journal of Youth and Adolescence, 14*, 389–399.

Hyde, J. S., & Fennema, E. (1990). *Gender differences in mathematics performance and affect: Results of two meta-analyses.* Paper presented at the meeting of the American Educational Research Association, Boston, MA.

Kerr, B. A. (1995). *Smart girls: A new psychology of girls, women, and giftedness.* Scottsdale, AZ: Gifted Psychology Press.

Kerr, B. A., & Cohn, S. J. (2001). *Smart boys: Talent, manhood, and the search for meaning.* Scottsdale, AZ: Great Potential Press.

Kimball, M. M. (1989). A new perspective on women's mathematics achievement. *Psychological Bulletin, 105*, 198–214.

Koehler, M. S. (1990). Classrooms, teachers, and gender differences in mathematics. In E. Fennema & G. C. Leder (Eds.), *Mathematics and gender.* (pp. 128–148). New York: Teachers College Press.

Maccoby, E. E., & Jacklin, C. N. (1974). *The psychology of sex differences.* Stanford, CA: Stanford University Press.

Murray, C. (August 22, 2005). The inequality taboo. www.commentary-magazine.com.

Olszewski-Kubilius, P., & Grant, B. (1996). Academically talented women and mathematics: The role of special programs and support from others on acceleration, achievement, and aspirations. In K. Arnold, K. D. Noble & R. F. Subotnik (Eds.), *Remarkable women* (pp. 281–294). Cresskill, NJ: Hampton Press.

Pallas, A. M., & Alexander, K. L. (1983). Sex differences in quantitative SAT performance: New evidence on the differential coursework hypothesis. *American Educational Research Journal, 20,* 15–182.

Peterson, P. L., & Fennema, E. (1985). Effective teaching, student enjoyment in classroom activities, and sex-related differences in learning mathematics. *Journal of Research in Mathematics Education, 13,* 66–136.

Pintrich, P. R., & Blumenfeld, P. C. (1985). Classroom experience and children's self-perceptions of ability, effort, and conduct. *Journal of Educational Psychology, 77,* 646–657.

Reis, S. M. (2002). Internal barriers, personal issues, and decisions faced by gifted and talented females. *Today Magazine, (25)*1, 14–28.

Reis, S. M. (1998). *Work left undone: Choices and compromises of talented females.* Mansfield Center, CT: Creative Learning Press.

Reis, S. M., & Kettle, K. (1994). *Project Parity evaluation.* Unpublished evaluation report. Storrs, CT: University of Connecticut Neag Center for Gifted Education and Talent Development.

Rejskind, F. G., Rapagna, S. O., & Gold, D. (1999). Gender differences in children's divergent thinking. *Creativity Research Journal, 5,* 165–174.

Renzulli, J. S., & Reis, S. M. (1991). The reform movement and the quiet crisis in gifted education. *Gifted Child Quarterly, 35,* 26–35.

Renzulli, J. S., & Smith, L. H. (1974). *Learning styles inventory.* Wethersfield, CT: Creative Learning Press.

Rogers, P. (1990). Thoughts on power and pedagogy. In L. Burton (Ed.), *Gender and mathematics: An international perspective* (pp. 38–46). London: Cassell.

Rubin, J. Z., Provenzano, F. J., & Luria, Z. (1974). The eye of the beholder: Parents' view on sex of newborns. *American Journal of Orthopsychiatry, 44,* 512–519.

Sadker, M., & Sadker, D. (1994). *Failing at fairness: How America's schools cheat girls.* New York: Charles Scribner's Sons.

Siegle, D., & Reis, S. M. (1998). Gender differences in teacher and student perceptions of student ability and effort. *Gifted Child Quarterly, 42,* 39–47.

Silverman, L. K. (1993). Social development, leadership, and gender issues. In L. K. Silverman (Ed.), *Counseling the gifted and talented* (pp. 291–327). Denver, CO: Love.

Stallings, J. (1985). School, classroom, and home influences on women's decisions to enroll in advanced mathematics classes. In S. Chipman, L. Brush, &

D. Wilson (Eds.), *Women and mathematics: Balancing the Equation* (pp. 199–224). Hillsdale, NJ: Erlbaum.

Stone, E. (1992). *The Hunter College campus school for the gifted: The challenge of equity and excellence.* New York: Teachers College Press.

Subotnik, R. F., & Strauss, S. M. (1995). Gender differences in classroom participation and achievement: An experiment involving Advanced Placement calculus classes. *Journal of Secondary Gifted Education, 6,* 77–85.

Webb, N. M., & Kenderski, C. M. (1985). Mathematics small group interactions among high ability learners: Gender differences in small group interaction and achievement in high- and low-achieving classes. In L. C. Wilkerson & C. B. Marrett (Eds.), *Gender influences in classroom interaction* (pp. 209–236). New York: Academic Press.

9

"We've Always Done It This Way"
Single-Sex Classes in Kenya

Robin J. Kohl

Flapping his wings, the rooster ascended in a sudden blurred movement from the floor to the tabletop. Slowly, quietly, carefully, he picked his way down the row of classroom tables, oblivious to the dated computer keyboards that cluttered his path. The female students, seated at wooden tables that formed a *U*, remained unfazed, paying not a whit of attention to their guest. As they continued their focused discussion on the topic at hand, the rooster hopped to the floor, slowly circled the room, and left as unceremoniously as he had come.

The students, top academic performers at a selective all-girls school in Kenya, were reserved and soft-spoken as they discussed their educational experiences. Despite the lack of classroom resources and modern facilities (and the occasional barnyard visitor), these students enthusiastically discussed their journeys in studying and learning. Continued reports of the paucity of American students, and particularly female students, proficient in the maths and sciences at the university level, along with revelations of gender inequities in student performance (Ginsburg et al., 2005; Van Langen, Bosker, & Dekkers, H., 2006).), raise the question of how the education of secondary youth in other countries encourages and prepares them to pursue advanced study in these subjects. Particularly of interest is the experience of females in the maths and sciences, which is typically delivered in single-sex schools. Although a lower percentage of the total population of females attends secondary school in Kenya (Branyon, 2005; Kamotho, 2002), their course of study parallels that of the males. In a country with far fewer resources than most Western nations, what contributes to the success of these females in completing secondary courses of study in the maths and sciences that are as rigorous as their male counterparts' and enables them to earn degrees at domestic and foreign universities in these and related disciplines?

In contrast to the American system of high school study, where students are able to graduate with no advanced math or science classes, the Kenyan Ministry of Education mandates a national curriculum for secondary schools (Kenya Institute of Education, 2002).

The curriculum is clearly organized to reflect the national goals and objectives of secondary education; specific objectives are published in every subject area for each of the 4 years of instruction. In the maths and sciences, the curriculum has much in common with schools in the United States, and yet there is more integration and depth in the subjects studied in Kenyan schools. For example, all students take physics and chemistry for 4 years, integrating the material typical of a college-level introduction course (Kenya Institute of Education, 2002).

Another clear difference in the Kenyan educational system is the hierarchical nature of its schools. The public school system is divided into three types of schools: district, provincial, and national. Seventeen national schools are designed to educate the top students, enrolling approximately 1.5% of secondary students. At the end of elementary school, every student takes the Kenya Certificate of Primary Education (KCPE) Examination. These scores are ranked and published, and the best students vie for seats in schools with varying levels of prestige. The schools are ranked and widely known by the achievement levels of their students. When students take the KCPE, they note a preference for a national school and a provincial school. When exam results are released, the national schools choose their students first, based solely on academic achievement on the KCPE. Students who do not score high enough to attend a national school are then chosen by the provincial schools. Many of the provincial schools show achievement levels that are almost as high as the national schools; provincial schools serve approximately 20% of secondary school students. Although the system is public, the schools charge fees, which sometimes prohibit even the brightest students from attending the best schools. Students who do not attend the highest-ranked schools attend their local district schools.

Almost all of the nation's provincial and national secondary schools serve students of a single gender, since they are public boarding schools. The structure of the system practically dictates that the top-performing schools will be single-sex institutions, since they are basically magnet schools, drawing the highest achieving students from all over the country. In addition, even families who live only a few miles away expect their children to board at the school, since the lack of a family car would render necessary the use of public transportation, which is too expensive and time consuming for a daily commute. Interestingly, the recent decision by Nakuru High School, Kenya's only coeducational national school, to segregate its students by gender as part of a plan to improve its performance in national examinations is testament to the widespread belief that single-gender schooling is most effective. ("Split Imminent," 2006). Since the majority of the high-achieving students go to single-gender schools, and these schools recruit the most talented teachers and have the most resources, it is difficult to determine what the effect of the single-gender setting has on overall academic performance. Nonetheless, when the national schools are compared, the fact that the single coeducational school has been performing the most poorly overall of the top tier of schools raises interest in the question.

In an exploratory effort to gain an understanding of the high school experiences of females in single-sex schools, high achieving students (N = 15) from three national girls' secondary schools were interviewed. The five highest-achieving students from each school, identified by their principals through test scores, agreed to participate. In each instance, the group of five girls discussed their early school memories, motivation, study habits, social relationships, and future plans. Shy and unassuming, the students were eager to learn about the reasons for these conversations and willing to share their thoughts. From the perspective of an American educator, the results were fascinating.

The experiences of female students at a prestigious single-sex secondary school are especially interesting in light of the educational obstacles that are faced by Kenyan girls. Poverty forces many daughters to forgo school in order to help with financial burdens, and fathers in tribal areas may offer their daughters as early as ages 9 or 10 in marriage to obtain the dowries. Along with the traditional reasons for training girls in the domestic arts, the male preference for subservient females and the sheer cost of educational fees keeps many girls from access to secondary schooling and university (Branyon, 2005; Kamotho, 2002).

The girls who gathered for discussion were indistinguishable with regard to their socioeconomic status. All wore the same uniforms, similar hairstyles, and shy smiles. In response to questions regarding whether the students enjoyed school, the girls were perplexed. School is simply a fact of life; the best hope for a future in Kenya lies in obtaining a good education. As a result, the goal of all students is to excel in their schoolwork in order to be able to support themselves and their families in the future. Education is a means to survival, not particularly something that one enjoys. Despite the confusion on this point, the school in general was full of students who appeared to enjoy their studies, focused during class, yet playful and friendly at breaks.

Recognizing the underlying importance of an education in the Kenyan culture, it is not surprising that all 15 of the girls indicated exams as the chief motivator for studying. Exams determine the future of the students from the time they are in elementary school, and they become increasingly important as students vie for small numbers of slots available in the country's six universities as well as for the limited scholarships available from foreign schools (Toyoda, 1997).

From the time a Kenyan child begins school, adults note and discuss which students are the most clever. Early on, the adults verbalize their high expectations and hopes for these children to advance in the educational system and eventually obtain positions that will ensure financial success, a source of both pride and provision for the extended family. Since individual student test scores are posted at the end of each school year, the academic progress of the community's children is very often common knowledge. Throughout the school experience, the students are accustomed to being ranked by their examination scores, and classmates at the girls' secondary schools are keenly aware of who among them are the brightest girls in each class.

In addition to the power of the exam to motivate, Kenyan girls have other reasons to work hard at their studies. Surprisingly, 11 of the 15 girls cited their fathers as their primary source of motivation to do well in school. Some indicated a positive encouragement, while others feared his disapproval if they were to perform poorly, but all spoke of their fathers with obvious affection. With a wide smile, one student shared, "I dare not drop below number 2 in the class, or I will have a lot of explaining to do. I am happy with number 2, because there is another girl in the class that I have never been able to defeat, but oh, if I drop to 3 or 4, he will wonder what has happened that I have been defeated! It would be a great shame, because the other girls in the class know who is the most clever, and we must keep our places, or they will have many things to say about it."

Of the end-of-semester reports, she said, "When my father arrives, I should be standing there with the grade report in my hand. He will first look at it before we drive away, even though the other parents tell him he could wait until we arrive home. I know what kind of lecture would be coming if I do not perform well."

And yet, for all her talk about her father being upset, she shared these stories with a warm affection and impishness in her voice. It was clear that she wanted her father's approval, but she did not fear his anger. Only two girls mentioned that their mother was a source of motivation, but perhaps that was because the mothers stood with the fathers as partners or supporters of the academic encouragement. A student noted, "Even though my mom is a teacher, she behaves as if everything did not center on education. When my father leaves during the week to work [during school breaks], he leaves an assignment for every day, and on the weekend, he grades them. If he is there, you need to be studying. When he is gone, my mother is happy if you warm yourself by the fire and roast some corn and laugh together."

The overwhelming personal influence of fathers and their educational views and encouragement is striking in the lives of these young Kenyan women. In contrast, although studies link American girls' enrollment in challenging courses to the influence of parents and a supportive home environment (Gavin, 1996), female enrollment in advanced math in the United States is also closely tied to SES (socieconomic status), mother's educational level, and student plans to attend graduate school (Reynolds & Conaway, 2003). An examination of the educational levels of the Kenyan girls' mothers would be informative. Perhaps, though unseen by the girls, mothers exert some silent influence on achievement levels.

Of course, SES is a factor in Kenya as well, since educated parents who hold lucrative positions will want to provide the best educations possible for their children (Miako, 1998; Onsomu, Kosimbei, & Ngware, 2005). As in the United States, parents with resources will provide additional opportunities and materials for intellectual growth, along with strong support for learning. Nonetheless, through the universal exam, opportunities exist for poverty-stricken students of merit (if they can raise school fees) to take their places alongside students from higher socioeconomic classes.

Although it appears in this study that much of the girls' motivation was extrinsic, emanating from a desire to please their fathers, at least half mentioned that they spend time studying because they want to know the information; they want to master the content. A few more shyly acknowledged that they enjoy the competition, trying to beat the other girls in a friendly rivalry. Although they know that they may be helping a classmate who is in direct competition against them, the girls often study together.

"It is the best feeling when you know you have done your best, and you have defeated the others. It is a sad feeling when you know that you have been defeated! The girls know who is clever and when someone is defeated, the others are sad for them."

The girls root for one another and have developed a sense of community (Haag, 1998); they have a tacit sense of respect for other bright females and freely acknowledge and expect that certain students will outperform others in the academic arena. The negative stereotypes of intellectuals found in Western literature are nonexistent here (Moon & Ray, 2006), yet the girls' positive reports parallel those in the United States, where students indicate that they enjoy the social environment and challenge of working with intellectual peers (Lubinski & Benbow, 2000). This sense of community and common purpose is consistent with comments by female students in single-sex schools in England as well as the United States (Robinson & Gillibrand, 2004; Monaco & Gaier, 1992; Sadker & Sadker, 1994).

In keeping with the economic issues that underlie the importance of education, the students had surprisingly common career goals, although most expressed them as a choice of one or two occupations. More than half of the girls indicated that they would like to be lawyers, while about a third mentioned becoming economists or businesswomen. Only two had entertained the possibility of becoming teachers, despite their success in academics and apparent love of learning. Possibly one of the reasons for this is that, while female teachers in Kenya are typical at the preschool level, male teachers outnumber women significantly at the high school and university level (Branyon, 2005). Females focused on academic achievement would possibly prefer to teach at those higher levels and subconsciously perceive that positions may not be available, since those posts are traditionally held by men.

The major reason given for the choice of the most popular careers, law and business, was that the potential earnings would be sufficient to provide for their financial needs. In a country racked by poverty, unemployment, and AIDS, logic dictates that physical needs might overshadow passionate pursuits of the mind (Huitt, 2004). For females, marriage was once considered the route to financial stability and physical well-being, but the modernization of Kenya and the AIDS epidemic is beginning to change that expectation, particularly in the urban areas (Mukudi, 2002). The once common practice of polygamy is less appealing to women and harder to sustain financially for men, and AIDS has decimated much of the population. Although there has been a push in recent years to educate the population about HIV/AIDS, including prominently displayed billboards even in rural areas, it is still a subject that is taboo in most circles. Indeed, these students specifically mentioned that they were avoiding young men and planned to postpone marriage to pursue careers and take care of their immediate families. Although the girls' families made it clear that they did not want them to socialize with young men, the subject of sexual activity or HIV/AIDS was not openly discussed in their homes. The implicit understanding among the girls was that to become involved with young men was to flirt with an early death.

Since education is so highly regarded as a way to insure future security, and competition is fierce for limited access to higher education, the students' chief goal is to do well on exams. To accomplish this goal, the girls reported that they studied from dawn to dusk, if not more. A third of the girls reported spending between 6 and 7 hours per day *outside of class* studying. The other two-thirds reported studying for over 7 hours per day. As one young lady put it, "My job here is to do well in school. If I am not in class or doing my chores, then I am expected to be studying. I get up early and study before breakfast, and I study in the evening late into the night. If I have a free moment, I am studying a book. It is the same on the days off from school."

This is in stark contrast to international reports of students who spend an average of 2.8 hours per day studying (TIMSS, 1999).

The dedication of these Kenyan schoolgirls to learning, despite the obstacles that face them, is inspirational. Although their experiences may be unique in that the constraints of their educational system dictate much of their school environment, there are similarities that transcend boundaries. In an all-girls school, they are not distracted by relationships with males, purposely postponing them at least until they complete high school. Like their high-achieving counterparts in the United States, the girls are motivated by competition, their families, and their futures, and they work collaboratively with their classmates with a goal toward increased learning for all.

One of the clear implications here is that girls in a single-gender setting have positive relationships and encourage one another to reach high academic goals. Although the national course of study compels them to continue in advanced math and science classes, they do so avidly and with no thought that those subjects are somehow difficult for girls or not interesting to girls. Could this single-gender arrangement be a factor that would contribute to higher achievement levels for females in the United States as well? Might the camaraderie and collaborative—albeit occasionally competitive—relationships among female students be a key to encouraging the study of disciplines that are traditionally less common for women in higher education?

Of course, the societal opportunities and expectations of females in the United States are much different than those in Kenya, but the fact remains that the Kenyan girls, with far fewer resources, successfully study advanced courses in the maths and sciences. We as educators can glean from their experiences and use that knowledge to further encourage our own girls' advanced study of mathematics and science. Perhaps we have been asking the wrong question. Rather than *Can single-sex settings increase academic achievement?* perhaps it should be *Can single-sex settings increase female enrollment in advanced coursework?* Whether or not single-sex arrangements increase academic achievement, which is unclear at best (Harvey, 1985; Riordan, 1990; Robinson & Gillibrand, 2004; Young & Fraser, 1992), the evidence shows that for females, there is a strong sense of community that is established in these settings (Haag, 1998; Monaco & Gaier, 1992; Sadker & Sadker, 1994; Streitmatter, 1998). Perhaps it is this intangible connection that would encourage more girls to take advanced math and science classes, and that would be reason enough to mandate the option of single-gender classes in our schools.

REFERENCES

Branyon, J. B. (2005). Education for all: Gender equity in Kenya. *Delta Kappa Gamma Bulletin, 71*(2), 8–11.

Gavin, M. K. (1996). The development of math talent: Influences on students at a women's college. *Journal of Secondary Gifted Education, 7*, 476–486.

Ginsburg, A., Cooke, G., Leinwand, S., Noell, J., & Pollock, E. (2005). *Reassessing U.S. international mathematics performance: New findings from the 2003 TIMSS and PISA*. Washington, DC: American Institutes for Research.

Haag, P. (1998). Single-sex education in grades K–12: What does the research tell us? In *Separated by sex: A critical look at single-sex education for girls* (pp. 13–38). Washington, DC: AAUW.

Harvey, R. J. (1985). Science in single-sex and mixed teaching groups. *Educational Research, 27*(3), 179–182.

Huitt, W. (2004). Maslow's hierarchy of needs. *Educational Psychology Interactive*. Valdosta, GA: Valdosta State University. Retrieved May 25, 2006 from http://chiron.valdosta.edu/whuitt/col/regsys/maslow.html.

Kamotho, K. (2002, March 8). Kenyan women turn down study opportunities. *The Times Higher Education Supplement*, 15.

Lubinski, D., & Benbow, C. P. (2000). States of excellence. *American Psychologist, 55*, 137–150.

Kenya Institute of Education. (2002). *Secondary education syllabus*. Vols. 1–4. Nairobi: Kenya Institute of Education.

Miako, S. (1998). *Gender vs. socio-economic status and school location differences in grade 6 reading literacy in five African countries*. Harare, Zimbabwe: Southern African Consortium for Monitoring Educational Quality.

Monaco, N. M., & Gaier, E. L. (1992). Single-sex vs. coeducational environment and achievement in adolescent females. *Adolescence, 27*(107), 579–594.

Moon, S. M., & Ray, K. (2006). Personal and social talent development. In F. A. Dixon & S. M. Moon (Eds.), *The Handbook of Secondary Gifted Education* (pp. 249–280). Waco, TX: Prufrock.

Mukudi, E. (2002). Gender and education in Africa. *Comparative Education Review, 46*, 2.

Onsomu, E. N., Kosimbei, G., & Ngware, M. (2005) *Impact of gender and socioeconomic factors on primary education performance in Kenya: Empirical evi-*

dence. Harare, Zimbabwe: Southern African Consortium for Monitoring Educational Quality.

Reynolds, N. G., & Conaway, B. J. (2003). Factors affecting mathematically talented females' enrollment in high school calculus. *Journal of Secondary Gifted Education, 14*, 218–228.

Riordan, C. (1990). *Girls and boys in school: Together or separate?* New York: Teachers College Press.

Robinson, W. P. & Gillibrand, E. (2004). Single-sex teaching and achievement in science. *International Journal of Science Education, 26*(6), 659–675.

Sadker, M., & Sadker, D. (1994). *Failing at fairness: How our schools cheat girls*. New York: Simon & Schuster.

Split imminent at country's only mixed national school. (2006, February 21). *Daily Nation*, A1.

Streitmatter, J. (1998). Single-sex classes: Female physics students state their case. *School Science and Mathematics, 98*(7), 369–375.

Toyoda, T. (1997). Kenya 1975–1995: An introductory note on educational expansion. *Assessment in Education: Principles, Policy, and Practice, 4*(1), 87–91.

TIMSS. (1999). *Trends in international mathematics and science study, 1998–1999*. Amsterdam: International Association for the Evaluation of Educational Achievement. Retrieved May 25, 2006 from http://nces.ed.gov/timss/results.asp.

Van Langen, A., Bosker, R., & Dekkers, H. (2006). Exploring cross-national differences in gender gaps in education. *Educational Research and Evaluation, 12*(2), 155–177.

Young, D., & Fraser, B. (1992, April). Sex differences in science achievement: A multilevel analysis. Paper presented at the American Educational Research Association.

10

Now What?
Practical Implications

Karen B. Rogers

The previous chapters of this book tell us both the advantages and disadvantages of placing middle school learners in single-sex or mixed classrooms for their learning. The contributors to this book describe their research experiences in light of other research. In this chapter, we conclude with a short summing-up of practices regarding single-sex classes that have been found to work *in practice* and present a set of recommendations for implementing these practices as well as where to go next in research and advocacy.

WHAT WE HAVE LEARNED

Title IX legislation does not restrict the implementation of single-gender classrooms in American schools.

Spielhagen, Ferrara, and Marks and Burns cited the growing numbers of public schools that have instituted these classes in the name of improved performance, spurred on by the No Child Left Behind performance requirements. Although federal mandates should not be the primary impetus for developing single-sex classrooms, it is interesting that educators have moved toward this management option more frequently when there is a perceived push to raise achievement. Certainly this was the case with

McCotter's description of a school that chose to institute these classes because the school did not meet AYP standards. Interestingly, single-sex classes were put into place to aid the learning of struggling learners, and little notice has been taken of their potential impact on bright learners. Spielhagen, for example, explained the lack of consistent improvement in academics in her school study by the fact that high achievers were placed in the mixed classes. McCotter's Zasha was moved from her single-sex class when her academic abilities were discovered. Correspondingly, the one study that tried to report ability-related differences (chapter 5) found no actual differences in achievement in math and science whether gifted students were placed in single-sex or mixed classes: They did equally well and considerably better than other students did. However, of more import in Rogers's study were the improvements in self-direction, self-regulation, and engagement in task-involved rather than ego-involved activity when high-ability students were placed in single-sex classes. Equity in assignment to single-sex classrooms must apply to children of all ability levels in our nation's current push to improve school success for all.

Boys interact differently in single-sex and mixed class placements. Furthermore, boys react within single-sex classrooms in considerably different ways than do girls in these classrooms.

Marks and Burns and Rogers both found that boys were not particularly happy with single-sex classes. While Marks and Burns were able to document that only 15 of the students in their initial group were willing to continue in single-sex classes in the second year, they suggested that boys were concerned about their emerging sexuality and feared a push toward "being gay" as the reason for not continuing. Rogers's interviews with a focus group of single-sex class boy participants as well as her classroom observations indicated that boys' concerns about single-sex classes were that the girls were getting further ahead academically and they wanted the girls to help them out with "looking good," "giving out the correct answers in class," and "helping with homework." McCotter documents the "pecking order" that was created in the single-sex boys' classes in her study. The older boys took to competing with the teacher for class leadership. There was resistance to learning and task expectations, there was a decline in achievement among the 8th-grade boys in the study, and there was evidence of mistrust and unwillingness to cooperate. There were also concerns raised about bullying and competition at higher levels in single-sex classes. Spielhagen found the competition to be a positive motivator, but noted that the boys in her single-sex setting tended to "act tougher." Hence, the tendency toward bullying may increase when boys do not have the socializing (mediating) influence of girls in their classroom. Interestingly, however, Ferrara reports that the instances of discipline referrals were markedly reduced among boys in single-sex classes for most offenses, including class disruption, lack of cooperation, tardiness, and disrespect to peers. Thus, the question remains: Were the perceptions of boys about peer behavior in single-sex classes accurate in the face of the quantitative evidence supplied by Ferrara?

Girls interact differently in single-sex and mixed class placements and the interactions are consistently more positive in single-sex settings.

Marks and Burns and Rogers found that girls were very satisfied with what went on in their single-sex classes. For Marks and Burns, the fact that 75% of the initial 100 students wished to continue in single-sex classes in the succeeding year was evidence of this. Rogers's observations showed the remarkable cooperative leadership that developed of its own accord in the 7th-grade girls' science and math classes, not to mention their petition to allow these classes to continue in the school, signed by every girl in the class. Even McCotter's story of the adversarial relationship that occurred between the 8th-grade girls and their teachers indicated the group cohesiveness that had been established within the single-sex setting. McCotter's case study of the emergence of leadership in Zasha is more than a case study of one. The focus on academics, task orientation, and the enjoyment of learning described in this chapter echo what Marks and Burns, Spielhagen, Rogers, and Kohl document about girls' behaviors. In the case of girls' behavior, Ferrara found remarkable reductions in disciplinary referrals for girls in single-sex classes: class disruptions, tardiness, lack of cooperation, and insubordination. The news for girls in single-sex settings is good, both in previous research and in the studies described in this book.

Middle school student choice of classroom setting (single-sex or mixed) is critical when considering the affective outcomes of school.

In three chapters of this book, there were stories of how the single-sex classes were established. Marks and Burns described a serendipitous class schedule, which was supposedly random but actually resulted in all-boys' and all-girls' teams, an opportunity they used to their advantage. In another chapter, Rogers, using a government grant, was able to randomly assign 7th-grade students to treatment (single-sex) or control (mixed) groups within a single team in a middle school. In the third instance, Mc-Cotter described a brainstorming session among school educators when AYP results were substandard, resulting in an imposed "intervention" of single-sex classes. In a fourth study, Kohl describes how the structure of higher-quality schooling in Kenya requires single-sex schools for women if they are to receive a college preparatory education. Countering this were two chapters in which students and their families *did* have a choice to participate in either single-sex or mixed classrooms. The affective outcomes seemed to differ depending on how the students were placed. For Spielhagen, students were happy with their single-sex classes; both boys and girls felt they could be themselves in these classes and were free of the distractions (boys' view) and teasing (girls' view) that they experienced in mixed classes. Teachers reported that both boys and girls were comfortable in single-sex classes, and that girls in particular responded more freely and frequently in single-sex classes. In Ferrara's study, there were significantly fewer instances of behaviors requiring disciplinary referral with both boys and girls in single-sex classes. Her teachers also reported more comfort for both boys and girls when they were in single-sex classes.

Higher academic achievement can be an outcome of single-sex classrooms, but cannot be guaranteed as a sure outcome of single-sex class placement alone.

Although many of these experiments were set up to aid with academic improvement, the academic outcomes from study to study were inconsistent. There were improvements in Marks and Burns's, Spielhagen's, and

Rogers's students in single-sex placements, in terms of either better grades or better achievement test scores. Certainly for the Kenyan girls studied by Kohl there was a difference academically, if only by the choice students could make if they wanted to succeed in school. In McCotter's study also, improved grades were reported for the girls in single-sex classes. However, for Ferrara, test scores did not change even when school marks improved slightly. Perhaps the academic results would have been more definitive if any of the studies had gone for longer than 2 or 3 years, but in most cases measures were taken at the end of one semester, or at most one year. One must be concerned that even if self-efficacy and time on task were improved in the first year, it might take considerably longer for these behaviors to translate into better academic performance.

Age and developmental level can affect the success of single-sex classroom placement to some extent.

Eighth grade seemed to be a landmark year for the studies reported in this book. By 8th grade, the positive affective and academic outcomes of the earlier middle school years seem to have diminished. The best results were with the youngest students, and the closer these learners came to true adolescence, the less willing they were to engage in single-sex classes and the less anxious they were to avoid disciplinary referrals. This was when the mob mentality confronted teachers in McCotter's study. Perhaps as older middle school students begin to seek their own identity and uniqueness, bonding with others of the same sex exclusively is not perceived as so useful as searching between both genders. One wonders, however, if the benefits reported here for grades 6 and 7 in middle school should be happening much earlier in the school years, perhaps even as early as the primary grades, if the full affective and academic benefits of single-sex classrooms are to be realized.

Teachers teach differently in single-sex settings, regardless of their preparation to do so.

For the studies chronicled in this volume, little professional development was provided. For Marks and Burns, the lack of time was the issue. For Rogers, the teachers who taught both science and math in both classroom conditions had done private reading and were motivated to engage, but had been provided with little professional development. Likewise for McCotter: The changes in administration attempted to support the teaching staff were inconsistent at best. In all of these cases, teachers reported that they taught differently in their single-sex classrooms. Teaching in all cases in these classrooms was less teacher-directed in that the teachers adjusted assignments, tasks, explanations, pacing, and project expectations to the different student permutations. In most of these cases, as described in some detail by Rogers, the teachers changed their style of presentation but not their content. Less explanation, more in-class time on routine tasks, and fewer homework expectations seemed to govern the teachers' work with the single-sex boys' math and science classes. More discussion, less in-class time on routine tasks, and more extensive work on assignments outside of school time so that more off-tasks and freewheeling discussions could take place during class seemed to be the story for single-sex girls' classes. The emergence of academic leadership among the girls was outlined by McCotter, in stark contrast to the competition and aggressive downplaying that took place among the boys. Spielhagen's studies revealed teachers who seemed to revel in the differences required of them and who became more convinced as time went on that teaching differentially to single-sex classes resulted in greater academic focus. Ferrara's careful analysis of questionnaire, interview, and observational data from the teachers in her study identified specific tips for teaching effectively in gender-specific classrooms. This "Teaching Tips" table will serve the field well as empirical research undertakes to establish just how effective each of these strategies may be across other schools and settings. Academic improvement is almost sure to follow once instructional differentiation for gender has been consistently applied. The teachers in the studies documented here were forced in most cases to react to the situations in which they were literally "thrown," rather than to work up to it, buy into it, and proactively acquire the knowledge and skills they would need to teach effectively in single-sex classes.

Administrative leadership has much to do with the success or lack of success when single-sex classes are implemented.

In two instances, the administrators took advantage of a given situation and implemented single-sex classes. Marks and Burns made a computerized fluke an opportunity to try it. That openness has to go a long way toward explaining the ultimate success of the venture. Likewise Rogers describes a principal who was willing to "try" the idea when a grant was written by two science and math teachers in her school to set up single-sex classes. Again, the administrator's support of the two teachers went far in the ultimate success of the implementation. On the other hand, the lack of promised funds once the implementation was underway, severely hampering hard-working teachers who were trying to do their best to differentiate for their single-sex classes of students, helps to explain less-than-stellar outcomes in McCotter's study. The lack of teacher preparation, when coupled with changes in administrative leadership and subsequent changes in priority, ultimately resulted in the withdrawal of single-sex classes when new administrators came in.

WHAT DO WE DO WITH WHAT WE HAVE LEARNED?

Offer the choice of single or mixed classes to students and families.

Those studies with the most positive affective outcomes from students took place in single-sex classes in which the students opted to participate. These students were more likely to "admit" their enjoyment of these classes and more likely to take the opportunities provided to them to take advantage academically. Zasha in McCotter's study is a prime example of this comfort and enjoyment, even to the point that she came back periodically to visit her single-sex classmates group when she was ultimately "promoted" to a higher-ability class in the second year. The students interviewed by Spielhagen attested to being able to be themselves and to feel comfortable that they would not be teased if they took learning too seriously in the single-sex class, unlike their assumptions that the teasing would be there in mixed classes. For those studies in this volume for which students had no choice of whether or not they would participate, the boys had a particularly difficult time adjusting to single-sex classes. The climate was more negative and more competitive, and frustrations were regularly voiced about "having" to be in these classes. When given the choice to continue in these classes, the boys dropped out in droves in both Marks and Burns's and Rogers's studies, yet in those schools where choice was provided, sufficient numbers of boys did choose to participate in the single-sex classes. It is interesting that class sizes were considerably smaller for mixed classes in Spielhagen's study when students were given the choice of participating in either single-sex or mixed classes. It is suspected that smaller class sizes would aid in academic improvement as well. Hence, single-sex and mixed/small class sizes should show stronger academic gains for all students regardless of the choice of class setting made.

Provide remedial support for boys–directly instruct them in cooperative learning and social skills development.

The biggest difference in behavior reported in several of the studies in this book was that boys behaved more boisterously in single-sex classes. They were not being "socialized" by the presence of girls in their classroom and therefore went in for more aggressive behaviors with the other boys in the class. In contrast, girls seemed to work together more cooperatively, with their own forms of leadership emerging from this working together. The principal in Rogers's study suggested that perhaps direct training for boys in how to work cooperatively and how to interact "appropriately" in single-sex classrooms might ameliorate the potential *Lord of the Flies* tendencies that seem to lurk beneath the surface of all-boy environments for learning. The key seems to be to give the single-sex classroom a chance to succeed for boys by providing the supports they might need to be active learners in such an environment, rather than eliminate the option because of misbehavior and too much testosterone in the air. It is critical that this be considered in light of the extraordinarily positive and consistent outcomes for girls in single-sex classes. If one must have both sexes participating in single-sex classes in order for them to be offered in a school, then when one sex does not do well, we should not be forced to withdraw the option for the other sex, which does thrive in such conditions.

Start early with single-sex settings.

The most positive outcomes, academically and affectively, for both sexes in single-sex classes came for grades 6 and 7. Results seemed to become cloudier for grade 8 students. Speilhagen is quite clear about the differences her teachers and students reported for the younger students and their subsequent success under single-sex conditions. Further research should ascertain just how early such classes should begin. Would that be in the primary or intermediate elementary years as opposed to starting this in middle school? Would the earlier time be particularly effective for boys such that their ability to learn cooperatively would be set into place much earlier?

Offer single-sex classes for academic areas that are problematic.

Spielhagen left us with many questions that need answering in further studies and research. She argued that there might be some academic areas for which single-sex groups are more effective. Certainly math and science achievement was enhanced by single-sex participation in Rogers's study, and Spielhagen was able to document several academic areas in which students did better when in single-sex settings. In one study described, all academic areas were provided with single-sex classrooms, while the nonacademic areas were mixed. Further research should focus on whether all academic single-sex classes are indeed superior in outcome to very specific content areas such as mathematics or language arts. Certainly the research of other countries, whether in Kenya in the current book or in English-speaking parts of the world in which a large proportion of the schooling options are in private schools (religious or nonreligious), has demonstrated differential academic gains across the board for single-sex schools, with single-sex girls' schools outperforming single-sex boys' schools, and both single-sex schools outperforming mixed schools. How applicable this is to the American situation, however, is up for question. The majority of our schools are public, which suggests that when private schools are selected there is an economic advantage accompanying outcomes. This may make the findings of single-sex schools less applicable to our increasingly diverse public schools in the United States.

Professional development is a must when single-sex classes are to be implemented.

Professional development is espoused in almost every study included in this volume, yet its dearth is also reported. If it were not for the individual efforts of the teachers in most of these studies to learn on their own or from their own experiences on the job, it would be difficult to assert that teacher training contributed at all to what success was reported in these studies. Certainly McCotter points to the lack of success overall in her study to the lack of promised resources for professional development. Marks and Burns spend much time talking about the professional development that would have been helpful and what difference it could have made to their outcome. Nonetheless, the research on professional development has consistently shown that when teachers are well trained in the reform they are to implement, they do implement it more successfully and consistently. Ferrara's instructional tips for teaching effectively in single-sex classes would be a good starting point for the specifics of professional development when schools begin to implement single-sex classes. Likewise, using Marks and Burns's protocol for introducing the single-sex class as a school reform would go far in ensuring implementation success.

In summary, Spielhagen has perhaps said it best in terms of how we need to go about making the best of what we know about single-sex classrooms:

> [D]o single-sex classes produce the desired results—that is, higher standardized test scores? Simply put, from the compilation of the studies examined in this volume, the answer is a resounding "Yes," "No," and "Maybe." While single-sex classes are not a panacea for the social ills that beset young adolescents and impact their academic performance, recent research suggests that such arrangements work for some students, boys and girls, in some academic areas. . . . Single-sex class arrangements seem to be most effective when related to the developmental needs of the students: the younger the student, the more likely that being in a single-sex class will be a positive experience. Second, in a public school environment, single-sex classes should be presented as optional to parents and students, with flexibility within the school day and over the student's middle school years.

About the Editor and Contributors

C. Sloan Burns, MEd, is director of a specialty high school for students gifted in the areas of mathematics and science. Prior to his present position he was an administrator on the high school level and taught mathematics also on the secondary level. Mr. Burns has presented at numerous conferences/workshops, most recently in San Antonio, Texas, entitled "Thinking Mathematically."

Margaret Ferrara, PhD, a generalist in curriculum and instruction at the K–12 level, serves as the department chair in Curriculum, Teaching, and Learning at the University of Nevada, Reno. Dr. Ferrara has an extensive background in research on single-gender education, models of teaching, and parent involvement.

Peter Ferrara, EdD, a retired school superintendent and researcher, serves as the CEO of Multiple Perspectives About Teaching, a research and evaluation corporation in Reno, Nevada. Dr. Ferrara and his wife, Margaret, are cocollaborators on single-gender and school improvement research.

Robin J. Kohl, PhD, is associate professor of education at Point Loma Nazarene University in San Diego, California, where she oversees clinical practice and teaches courses in assessment. Her career includes stints as teacher, gifted program coordinator, and principal. Her research interests are in the areas of international and gifted education and K–12/university partnerships.

Deborah E. Marks, PhD, is principal of a large high school in central Virginia and is an adjunct faculty member for a large urban university for the school of education. Prior to her present position she was a middle school principal, a supervisor of special education, and a teacher of elementary, middle, high school, and postsecondary education. Dr. Marks has been published in the areas of student participation and identification with school, school leadership, and school cultural norms.

Suzanne Schwarz-McCotter, PhD, is an associate professor of educational leadership at Montclair State University in Montclair, New Jersey. Her background is in instruction and leadership in middle school settings. Dr. McCotter's research interests include teacher reflection, professional development, and school culture. She is honored to have been the mentee and student of the book's editor, Dr. Spielhagen, since the age of 14.

Karen B. Rogers, PhD, is director of research at the Gifted Education Research, Resource and Information Centre (GERRIC) and professor of education in the Faculty of Arts and Social Sciences at the University of New South Wales in Sydney, Australia. She will be returning to the United States in 2008 as professor of gifted studies at the University of St. Thomas in Minneapolis, Minnesota. She has authored more than 100 journal articles, 20 book chapters, and 2 books, and has provided evaluations to more than 65 programs, curricula, and schools.

Frances R. Spielhagen, PhD, a career educator with more than 30 years experience in secondary schools, is currently an assistant professor of education at Mount Saint Mary College in Newburgh, New York. Dr. Spielhagen has also engaged in funded and published educational research, most recently as an AERA/IES Post-Doctoral Research Fellow at the College of William and Mary in Williamsburg, Virginia, and in conjunction with the Texas Higher Education Opportunity Project. She serves on the Advisory Board of the Gurian Institute and is president of the Sociology of Education Association.